THE EPISTLE TO THE HEBREWS

An Exposition

THE EPISTLE
TO
THE HEBREWS

An Exposition

by
CHARLES R. ERDMAN

PREFACE BY EARL F. ZEIGLER

THE WESTMINSTER PRESS

PHILADELPHIA

Published by The Westminster Press®
Philadelphia, Pennsylvania
PRINTED IN THE UNITED STATES OF AMERICA

PREFACE

A New Testament book of inestimable worth to the Christian religion is The Letter to the Hebrews. In length it is almost seven thousand words. Its authorship has never been identified with finality, and probably never will. As to the purpose of the letter, Biblical scholars are in substantial agreement. God "has spoken to us by a Son" who "reflects the glory of God and bears the very stamp of his nature." This Son is Jesus the Christ who, by his once-for-all sacrifice for sin, became the author of eternal salvation to all who believe in his name. He is "a merciful and faithful high priest in the service of God, to make expiation for the sins of the people." The message of the Hebrews is addressed to Christians who understand Judaism from personal experience, and who are in danger of abandoning their faith in Christ "leading you to fall away from the living God." Was it persecution, false teachers, or something else that created this danger? Whatever it was the author of the Hebrews piles testimony upon testimony to show that the Christian faith is the perfect and final religion; and that the sinner has unrestricted access to God through Jesus Christ. He has become the eternal and perfect High Priest. He is able "to sympathize with our weaknesses," because he is "one who in every respect has been tempted as we are, yet without sinning."

But the writer of a preface must not trespass on the territory allocated to an expositor. Dr. Charles R. Erdman is the expositor for this volume, and for the other sixteen in the series of Erdman commentaries on the complete New Testament. He combined the gifts of scholarship and pastoral ministries. A reading of his Introduction to the Hebrews will convince the student that he is not only well acquainted with the many phases of Biblical scholarship, but that he has unusual ability to organize and present his material. He uses the Introduction to alert the student to some of the problems that an interpreter must consider, but he also indicates clearly and convincingly his high appreciation of the Hebrews. His own personal experience of Christ becomes interwoven with his interpretation of the sacred writing.

After reading Dr. Erdman's Introduction, many students will find that it will be time-saving to read the entire text of the Hebrews. Rapid readers can do this silently in thirty minutes, vocally a little longer. The spell under which the unidentified author wrote; the inspiration that filled his soul; the burden he felt for men and women who had known Christ and were now wavering—something of this author's profound but practical ecstasy will be contagious. After this it will be time to spend many hours, even weeks, carefully studying the entire text with the skillful guidance of Dr. Erdman. To him have come church school teachers, pastors, members of study groups, individuals, college and seminary students by the thousands. A new set of type and plates has become necessary since this volume was first issued because the old are worn thin. This new paperback edition is sent forth to serve other students of the Word of God who will learn for themselves that they are surrounded by a great cloud of witnesses who are expecting them to "run with perseverance the race that is set before us, looking to Jesus."

EARL F. ZEIGLER

FOREWORD

Does Christianity claim to be the perfect and therefore the final form of religious belief? If so, on what grounds does it base so extraordinary a claim, and what consequent obligation rests upon its adherents to appreciate its full significance and to share its riches with the followers of other faiths?

Such are the questions raised and answered by the following fascinating letter, which consequently constitutes one of the most important documents in the literature of the world.

INTRODUCTION

"Free + unlimited access to God"

The Form of the Epistle

The Epistle to the Hebrews differs in form from all other epistles of the New Testament. Indeed, the question has been raised as to whether or not it is an epistle. It begins as an essay or treatise; it progresses as a sermon or homily; it ends as a letter.

That it does constitute a treatise of a high literary order, there can be no doubt. It presents a definite theme, which it develops with consummate skill. Its arguments are carefully composed and logically arranged. In no other portion of the New Testament is the treatment of a single subject so long sustained. Nor is any subject more vital to man. The great reality under discussion is that of the possibility of free and unrestricted access to God. It is the greatness of this theme, together with the power of its presentation, which makes this epistle supreme as an orderly statement of revealed truth.

Yet it is much more. It is an impassioned homily. The writer is not presenting a cold and formal discussion of religious dogma. He is writing with most practical intent. Every argument is the basis of an appeal. Again and again he interrupts his logical discussion to apply to his readers the truth he has established. He rebukes; he encourages; he warns; he pleads. A fire is burning in his soul. He is presenting vital realities to men who are in peril. Thus his production is an extended exhortation or sermon.

However, it is an epistle. It contains no opening salutation or address, yet its conclusion is of the form common in the letters of that day and quite in accord with those which are known to have come from the hands of Peter and of Paul. It is these closing greetings and personal messages which give a further note of reality to the discussion. The reader is made to feel that an ardent believer is writing to personal friends a message to express the immeasurable benefits he has experienced through faith in the Son of God.

THE AUTHOR

What was the name of this writer who had found such blessedness in Christ and who felt for certain of his fellow believers such deep concern? To this question no final answer has been given. For many centuries, by common consent, the epistle has been assigned to Paul. During the first four centuries no such agreement existed, and by most recent students the authorship of the apostle is denied.

Nowhere does the author name himself; nor is his identity disclosed. On the other hand, it was the invariable custom of Paul to begin his epistles with the mention of his own name and frequently to authenticate them by his personal signature. Paul quotes the Hebrew Old Testament; this writer quotes the Greek translation.

Those best able to judge declare that the language and style are not those of the apostle. The idiomatic and polished Greek, the precision of the phrases, the rhythm of the stately periods, are in striking contrast with the tempestuous and natural eloquence of Paul.

Nor is it quite exact to say that "the thoughts are those of the apostle." In substance they are. There is no contradiction of his teaching. There is, however, a different viewpoint and an altered emphasis. The person and work of Christ, the character of faith, the nature of salvation, the relation of law and gospel are presented under complementary but contrasted forms.

The most serious objection to the theory of Pauline authorship is found in the fact that the writer places himself among those to whom the gospel has been brought by men who heard the Lord and to whom the gospel has been attested by miracle (ch. 2:3), whereas Paul always maintains stoutly that he has received the gospel not "from men, neither through man," but "through revelation of Jesus Christ."

On the other hand, "if Paul did not write this epistle, no one knows who did." Even in the second century there were conflicting conjectures and traditions; but the author was regarded as unknown. The name of Barnabas was apparently the first to be advanced, and his claims have recently been revived. He fulfills many of the requirements. He belonged to the circle of Paul's friends and was acquainted with Timothy. (Ch. 13:23.) He was a man of ability and high character. He was a Levite and might be supposed to view the work of Christ under the terms of the Mosaic ritual. He came from Cyprus, where pure Greek was spoken, and was familiar with the church in Jerusalem and other circles of Hebrew believers. These facts, however, are far from decisive and it is the merest coincidence that Barnabas was known as a "Son of exhortation" (Acts 4:36), while the epistle is described as a "word of exhortation" (Heb. 13:22).

Many have ascribed the authorship of the epistle to Apollos. He was well qualified for such a task. Apollos was a Jewish Christian from Alexandria, a man of culture and wide learning, a man "mighty in the scriptures," "an eloquent man," who was "instructed in the way of the Lord," a man who "spake and taught accurately the things concerning Jesus." Surely such a man might have written this exposition of the saving work of Christ, so exquisite in its literary qualities and so continually moving in the sphere of the symbols and types of the Old Testament Scriptures.

Many other names have been proposed and eagerly supported. Among them are those of Luke, Silas, Peter, Clement, Aristion, and Philip the Evangelist. Quite recently the claims of Aquila and especially of Priscilla have been gallantly defended.

It is probably well to abide by the words of Origen, written seventeen centuries ago, concerning this epistle: "It was not without reason that the men of old time have handed it down as Paul's [that is, as substantially expressing his thoughts]; but who wrote the epistle God only knows certainly."

There is much that is attractive in the theory that the great apostle to the Gentiles addressed one specific message to those of his own nation who had accepted Christ, and there are features of the epistle which indeed might point to Paul as its author. However, the evidence for this theory seems to be lacking, and it is possible that the name of Paul became attached to the anonymous letter in order to secure its reception into the canon of sacred Scripture. That the letter merits such a place there can be no possible doubt. In view of its divine inspiration the human authorship of the epistle becomes a matter of little importance. That it does belong to the inspired writings, the Christian church of all the centuries has been convinced. As has been well said, "If we hold that the judgment of the Spirit makes itself felt through the consciousness of the Christian society, no book of the Bible is more completely recognized by universal consent as giving a divine view of the gospel, full of lessons for all time, than The Epistle to the Hebrews."

THE DESTINATION

The identity of the first readers of this epistle has been lost as completely as has that of its author. The title, "To the Hebrews," might indicate Jews, or Jewish Christians, or Hebrew-speaking Jewish Christians in general; but many expressions in the epistle, in addition to the personal references in the last chapter, make it certain that those addressed belonged to a particular local group or circle of Christian believers. Therefore, the title, "To the Hebrews," is not sufficiently definite to have been affixed by the writer. It may properly be regarded as "hardly more than a reflection of the impression produced on an early copyist."

If so, it was a correct impression. The epistle evidently was written for Hebrew Christians, although there are those who contend that the original readers were Gentiles. The whole argument, however, both in what it includes and what it assumes, indicates that both the writer and the readers were Jewish converts. One notable passage indicates how truly the whole atmosphere and outlook are Jewish. In referring to the entire redeeming work of Christ, it is stated that "not to angels doth he give help, but he giveth help to the seed of Abraham." Gentile nations, or the Gentile church, are not in the thought of the author. He does not specify that his readers were Jews; he implies this and makes no reference to Gentiles, or to the relations of Jewish and Gentile believers.

What, then, was the location of this group of Christians to whom the epistle was addressed? The most common and obvious conjecture is Jerusalem. Surely in that city there was a Christian society composed wholly of Jewish converts. In many respects the circumstances and experiences of these converts must have been similar to those which are stated or implied in the course of the epistle. There are, however, certain difficulties. It is improbable that the first reference to the readers would describe them as those who had received the gospel of Christ from "them that heard," if indeed they resided in the city where much of his teaching was done and where the church must have been composed largely of those who themselves had listened to his words. Then, too, the church in Jerusalem was memorable for its poverty, whereas the church addressed had been known widely for its charity (chs. 6:10; 10:34). Nor would the church at Jerusalem be open to rebuke for its failure and inability to understand and teach the gospel. (Ch. 5:12.) Moreover, in a letter sent to Jerusalem and dealing with the Jewish ritual it is strange that there is no reference to the Temple and its worship. Furthermore, if the church to which the writer belonged, and to which he wrote, was located in Jerusalem, or indeed in Palestine, it would have been natural for him to use the Aramaic language instead of the Greek, in which this epistle was composed.

Other proposed destinations are Asia Minor, Antioch, Alexandria, and Rome. Among recent critics the last named city is increasingly popular. It is admitted that little positive proof has been produced. There is possible significance in the final greeting, "They of Italy salute you" (ch. 13:24). This would seem to imply that the writer was in company with certain Italian Christians who may have been sending their salutation to friends in Rome. The conjecture, therefore, is that this letter was written by one who was addressing the Jewish portion of the church in Rome to which he himself belonged, or that possibly he wrote to a particular circle of the house churches to which Paul refers in the concluding chapter of his Epistle to the Romans.

The uncertain residence of the readers, however, is of much less importance than their past experiences and present condition; these are sketched with considerable definiteness. They were converts of long standing. Their faith had been inspired by men who were personally acquainted with the Lord; but since their conversion much time now had elapsed. In earlier days they had patiently endured pain and reproach. They had been exposed to the violence of the mob; they had suffered the loss of property; they had heard the jeers of malignant foes. They also had shown active sympathy for certain of their number who were imprisoned. Now their early enthusiasm had begun to fail. Their trusted leaders had fallen, possibly as martyrs. Their spiritual life was stagnant. They still believed in Christ as the Son of God and had no doubt as to the authority of Scripture; they still were within the church; they were "holy brethren, partakers of a heavenly calling"; they still showed their love by ministering to the saints; their prayers and cooperation were earnestly desired by the writer, who believed in their ultimate salvation. But they were immature, were making no progress, were neglecting their assemblies for worship, were feeling the sting of social ostracism, were threatened by the seductions of false teaching, were losing heart, were weary of their conflict against sin, and so were in actual peril of apostasy, of losing their faith in God, of turning hopelessly from Christ. It is these characteristics of the readers which make the epistle of such practical value in modern times. No matter where these Christians lived, their counterpart can be found in every land and age. Their spiritual condition is now only too common. Even where the claims of Christ and the truths of Scripture are not denied, there is found among Christians too frequently disillusionment, indifference, drifting, languor, weariness, practical unbelief. Whoever the original readers may have been, this epistle is addressed in a true sense to the church of the present day.

THE AIM AND METHOD

The purpose of the author is to prevent his readers from abandoning their faith in Christ. He is not attempting to keep them from relapsing into Judaism, as many have supposed. What he fears is a complete eclipse of faith, an actual apostasy, a "falling away from the living God." It is not the appeal of the Jewish ritual, or the attraction of an elaborate ceremonial, which is endangering their souls. It is rather the pressure of persecution, or the assaults of sin, or the peril of religious indifference. The writer aims, therefore, to set forth the incomparable glory of the person and work of Christ. He intends to show that the greatest sufferings are infinitely compensated by the supreme blessings secured by Christ for his followers. He desires his readers to realize these blessings. He would have them appreciate their privileges. He seeks to arouse their former zeal and maintain their loyalty by setting forth the true significance of their Christian faith.

He presents Christianity as the perfect and therefore the final religion, because it is the religion of free and unrestricted access to God. This access has been made possible by the atoning work of Christ. Through him men can draw near and can enjoy pardon and peace and fellowship with God. By his becoming man and by his redeeming death, Christ has secured the enjoyment of such immeasurable benefits. How great, then, must be the peril of turning away from him and of neglecting the salvation he has secured!

In order to make more clear the work of Christ, the writer compares Christianity with Judaism. He does not do so to disparage the latter. The institutions of Moses are treated, however, as types which find their fulfillment in Christ; they are the shadows which find their substance in him.

These ancient institutions had a definite place in the purpose of God. They were symbols which pictured to Israel great realities. The tabernacle and its service, on which the writer dwells with reverence and affection, did indicate the divine presence, the possibility of pardon, the provision for access and fellowship with God.

Yet these symbols were also types. To the ancient Hebrew they were pictures of spiritual realities; to the Christian they are prophecies which have been fulfilled in Christ. He is the true High Priest; he has offered the perfect sacrifice; he has entered the holy place "not made with hands"; he is the divine Intercessor who "is able to save to the uttermost."

To the writer of the Hebrews the ancient ritual belonged to this visible world, which is a world of shadows. Christ belongs to the unseen world, which alone is the world of realities. Thus throughout the entire epistle there is a continual contrast between the old and the new. The purpose is not to undervalue the old but to show how all the symbols and types of ancient Judaism are fulfilled in Christ, and are thus surpassed as the shadow is surpassed by the substance.

Thus the very theme of the epistle may be declared to be "the priesthood of Christ." The key word is "better," which is repeated again and again and is used to show the superiority of Christ to all mediators or deliverers or priests of the old dispensation.

However, as the writer unfolds the argument it becomes evident that he is demonstrating the superiority of Christianity, not only to Judaism but to all religions. He nowhere declares that it is the ultimate form of faith, but this he everywhere implies. As he displays the dignity of the great High Priest and the abiding efficacy of his atoning work, he is actually presenting Christianity as the one true religion, the hope of the whole world, the perfect and final revelation of God to man.

To most modern readers the use of the Mosaic ritual to illustrate the teaching of the author of the epistle may tend to obscure rather than to clarify his meaning. However, to one who wishes to profit by this epistle, it may be a real benefit to be required to review the earlier books of the Old Testament. Their full meaning cannot be appreciated aside from the light thrown upon them by the books of the New. However, it is also true that apart from the types and symbols of the Old Testament the full meaning of the atoning, redeeming, saving work of Christ can never be fully understood. Exodus and Leviticus have a new significance to the readers of The Epistle to the Hebrews, but so, too, the work of Christ as set forth in this epistle has a deeper meaning to those who find in the books of Moses prophetic types of the service and sacrifice of the great High Priest, Jesus, the Son of God.

What the author of the Hebrews actually did was to turn back the thoughts of his discouraged, listless, imperiled readers to the Scriptures to find in them an arresting, inspiring message concerning Christ. What the church needs today is to be turned again to the divine oracles to review their teaching concerning the Savior, who is himself the unique, the perfect, the final Word of God to man.

THE CONTENTS

It may appear unwise to interrupt the rhythmic and musical flow of the epistle by any attempt at literary analysis. Before and after a critical study such a composition should be read through from first to last, without any pause or comment. However, it does aid in the understanding and the appreciation of the epistle to trace the steps in the argument and to fix the thought successively on each significant paragraph.

The general outline is not difficult to discover. There are three clearly defined sections. The first contains doctrinal instruction (chs. 1:1 to 10:18); the second, practical exhortations (chs. 10:19 to 13:17); and the third, personal messages (ch. 13:18-25). This division, however, is not quite exact, as the first section contains three solemn exhortations or warnings and the second section contains much valuable instruction.

1. The general content of the opening chapters is a description of the person and work of Christ under the figure of a divine priesthood. He is superior to angels as a mediator between God and man, because, as the divine Son, he is himself the perfect revelation of God. (Ch. 1.) Therefore the readers are warned against neglecting the "salvation" provided by the Son. (Ch. 2:1-4.) Christ as a divine mediator is further superior to angels because he is the true representative of man, attaining supreme sovereignty by the way of incarnation and death. (Vs. 5-18.)

Christ is superior to Moses, as a son is superior to a servant. (Ch. 3:1-6.) Therefore, the readers are warned against the unbelief which was fatal to the followers of

Moses (vs. 7-19), and encouraged to seek that "rest" which Joshua and David did not secure for Israel and which yet awaits the true people of God (ch. 4:1-13). As Christ is not only the Moses but also the Aaron (ch. 3:1) of the new dispensation, believers are exhorted to hold fast their loyalty to him and to accept the access to the mercy seat which he provides (ch. 4:14-16).

Christ is, however, superior to Aaron, although it is true that both fulfilled the requirements of a high priest, namely, human sympathy and divine appointment. Through his grievous sufferings Christ fulfilled the first requirement. As to the second, the divine voice addressed him (Ps. 110:4) as "a priest . . . after the order of Melchizedek." (Heb. 5:1-10.)

superior to Aaron

Realizing that his teaching is becoming difficult to follow, the writer of the epistle interrupts his treatment of the high priesthood of Christ to deplore the spiritual dullness and immaturity of his readers (vs. 11-14); to remind them that to fail to advance is to be in danger of falling back; and to warn them against the deadly peril of apostasy (ch. 6:1-8). He encourages them to new hopefulness, and to imitation of the faith and patience of Abraham. Their assurances of obtaining the promises are greater than were his. Their hope is in heaven, whither Jesus has entered to make atonement, and also to provide access for those who follow him as their great High Priest. (Vs. 9-20.)

This priesthood of Christ is superior to that of Aaron, because it is "after the order of Melchizedek." The latter must have been greater than the Levitical priesthood, for Melchizedek received tithes from Abraham, the ancestor of Levi, and his priesthood is pictured as royal, universal, and supremely "unchangeable." So the priesthood of Christ is eternal; unlike the Aaronic priests he is free from infirmity, "made higher than the heavens" and "a Son, perfected for evermore." (Ch. 7.)

The preceding chapters have dwelt upon the personality of the High Priest; the writer now centers the thought upon his work, borrowing his figures from the ritual of the great Day of Atonement.   (Chs. 8:1 to 10:18.)

The scene of Christ's ministry, in contrast with that of the Aaronic priests, is not the earthly tabernacle but the heavenly, and the conditions of his ministry are, according to the prophecy of Jeremiah (Jer. 31:31-34), not those of the old covenant but of the new.   (Heb., ch. 8.)

In minute detail the writer describes the ancient sanctuary and refers to its elaborate ritual; but he shows that the very division of the Holy Place from the Holy of Holies and the restricted access allowed to the latter were indications that the real way of approach to God had "not yet been made manifest"; and he further shows that the ancient ordinances of service were temporary, material, typical, and could not "make the worshipper perfect."   (Ch. 9:1-10.)

By way of contrast he then describes the atoning work of Christ, first, in general (vs. 11-12), and then in its two essential features: (a) the necessary shedding of blood (vs. 13-22) and (b) the consequent entrance into the Holy Place (vs. 23-28).

Finally the writer brings his doctrinal teaching to a climax by fixing the thoughts upon the offering of the great High Priest.   He sets forth the sacrifice of Christ, contrasted with the typical and temporary sacrifices of the Mosaic law (ch. 10:1-4), showing, as stated in Psalm 40, that its essence is obedience to the will of God (Heb. 10:5-10).   The intrinsic value and abiding efficacy of the offering of Christ are emphasized as unlike the daily sacrifices of the old covenant.   (Vs. 11-14.)   This fact the author of the epistle establishes by the quotation from Jeremiah (Jer. 31:33), thus concluding his teaching with the testimony of Scripture.   (Heb. 10:15-18.)

2. The practical portion of the epistle (chs. 10:19 to 13:17) consists of exhortations, warnings, and appeals. These are based upon the superiority and finality of the

atoning work of Christ, set forth in the preceding chapters. They are designed to induce the readers to accept the privileges and to reveal the virtues which rightfully belong to the followers of Christ.

First of all comes the exhortation to the confident use of the access to God which Christ has provided. This touches the very heart of the epistle. It was voiced in an earlier chapter. (Ch. 4:14-16.) Here it is enlarged by a fuller statement of the provision for access, an earnest insistence upon steadfastness in faith and hope and upon the manifestation of love. (Ch. 10:19-25.)

This need of steadfastness is enforced by one of those solemn warnings against apostasy which are somewhat parenthetic in form and yet express the supreme purpose of the writer. Here the warning is specifically against willful sin and the peril of despising Christ and falling into the avenging hands of the living God. (Vs. 26-31.)

The readers are further encouraged to confident continuance in faith and hope and love by the remembrance of their courage and charity manifested in earlier days. (Vs. 32-39.)

The supreme stimulus to steadfast faith is furnished, however, by an eloquent and extended review of the achievements of faith as exemplified in the lives of the great heroes of the past. These are taken from the annals of Israel, beginning with the Patriarchs and coming down to the martyrs of Maccabean days. The recital reaches its climax in the example of Jesus himself, "the author and perfecter of our faith." (Chs. 11:1 to 12:2.)

Christians are further exhorted to the patient endurance of suffering viewed as the discipline of a loving Father. (Ch. 12:3-13.) They are further urged to lives of peace and purity, the latter in view of the irreparable consequences of unfaithfulness. (Vs. 14-17.)

The final warning against apostasy forms the very climax of the epistle. The great aim of the writer has been to encourage his readers fully to appreciate the message of God sent through his Son and to be true to that message in order that they may continue ever to enjoy fellowship with him. Here the solemn admonition is against refusing to hear the divine voice. The warning is enforced by contrasting the superior privileges of the new dispensation with those of the old and, further, by pointing out the peril of turning from him who speaks from heaven. (Vs. 18-29.)

This practical or hortatory section of the epistle closes with a statement of certain duties of the Christian life; first, those which are social (ch. 13:1-6); and then those which are religious (vs. 7-17).

3. The brief closing section is in a form appropriate to a letter, indicating that the composition is not merely a treatise but an epistle. First there is a request on the part of the writer for prayer in his behalf. (Vs. 18-19.) This is followed by a comprehensive benediction. (Vs. 20-21.) Last of all there are personal messages, and a familiar formula, "Grace be with you all." (Vs. 22-25.)

THE OUTLINE

I

I

DOCTRINAL: THE GREAT HIGH PRIEST AND HIS ATONING WORK

Heb. 1:1 to 10:18

[handwritten: God has spoken]

[handwritten: no attempt to undermine Old Testament laws + history]

A. THE GREAT HIGH PRIEST Chs. 1 to 7

1. THE SON AND THE PROPHETS Ch. 1:1-4

1 God, having of old time spoken unto the fathers in the prophets by divers portions and in divers manners, 2 hath at the end of these days spoken unto us in his Son, whom he appointed heir of all things, through whom also he made the worlds; 3 who being the effulgence of his glory, and the very image of his substance, and upholding all things by the word of his power, when he had made purification of sins, sat down on the right hand of the Majesty on high; 4 having become by so much better than the angels, as he hath inherited a more excellent name than they.

The first four verses form a majestic introduction to the epistle. They present its theme; they indicate its method; they give a summary of its doctrinal content. The thought is centered at once upon Christ, the divine Son of God. No mention is made of a human author or of the readers to whom he writes. Why should there be? The message concerns One through whom God speaks his final word to men. To this One the author points. He himself has no desire to be known. He wishes to reveal the matchless glory of his Lord in order that his readers may remain steadfast in their faith as they more fully appreciate the infinite privileges they enjoy as followers of Christ.

The aim of the writer is to show the superiority of Christ to all other mediators and messengers by whom God has revealed his saving grace to men. Specifically he is to contrast the revelation recorded in the Old Testament with that embodied in the person and work of Christ. He does not intend to disparage the old dispensation but to display the fuller meaning of the new.

Thus he begins with the statement, "God, having of old time spoken unto the fathers in the prophets by divers portions and in divers manners, hath at the end of these days, spoken unto us in his Son." The important point is this: "God . . . hath . . . spoken." Whether in the Old Testament or the New, it is the voice of God. Whether through the prophets or through a Son, the message is divine. The first affirmation is of the continuous nature of the revelation. Christianity was not designed as a break with Judaism; it was to be its completion, its fulfillment, its goal. He who spoke "of old time" to the fathers, that is, to believers of Old Testament days, spoke unto us who by faith are likewise his people.

It is true that some contrast is implied. "Old time" is distinguished from "the end of these days." The latter expression indicates that "the present age" finds its consummation not in ancient prophecy but in the atoning work of Christ, as the "age to come" is to be ushered in by the return of Christ.

The phrase, "By divers portions and in divers manners," may imply a revelation incomplete and temporary in comparison with the perfection and finality of that which is in the Son. "Divers portions" means in different pieces, here a little and there a little, in "broken parts," given progressively, as men were able to understand, but revealed fully and finally in Christ.

"Divers manners" refers to the different ways in which God spoke of old. Sometimes it was by a ritual, sometimes by a law, sometimes by a psalm, sometimes by a typical person or event, sometimes by a prophet. All these found their fulfillment, their embodiment, their substance in Christ.

However, these phrases do not discredit the older revelation. They show its richness, its fullness, its adaptation to the needs and the increasing spiritual intelligence of men. The contrast between the old and the new is drawn, however, in the phrases which are added as descriptive of the Son. This superiority of Christ as the embodiment of the divine revelation is set forth in six striking phrases:

a. "Whom he appointed heir of all things" points forward to the sovereignty yet to be exercised by Christ. This is the very goal of all human history. The Son is to be the universal Ruler, and this by virtue of his Sonship. Because he is the Son, therefore he is the Heir. (Gal. 4:7.) In his parable of the wicked husbandmen, Christ described himself as the Heir. When he became a man he claimed the inheritance. It will not be enjoyed fully until "the kingdom of the world is become the kingdom of our Lord, and of his Christ" (Rev. 11:15). The appointment, however, was made in the eternal purpose of God as recorded in Ps. 2:7-8; 110:1.

b. "Through whom also he made the worlds." The word "also" closely relates this with the preceding clause. The Heir of all things was their Creator; and, by implication, he was Heir of all things because he was their Creator. It was natural that God should give supreme and universal dominion to him who was his Agent in bringing all things into being. The term "worlds" is, literally, "ages," and is understood by some to denote "time worlds" or "world periods." Probably as used by the writer it has lost its sense of duration and means "the material universe" or simply "the world." However, it is quite possible that some relation to time was retained. The worlds were regarded as the outworking of God's purpose through the ages. The vastness of the universe is becoming, in recent years, more fully appreciated; but so, too, is the even more boundless expanse of time through which the divine plan has been unfolding. The statement here may indicate that Christ was the Creator of the universe in all its phases—past, present, and future.

c. The supremacy of Christ is further manifested in his divine person and his redeeming work. (V. 3.) In relation to "the worlds," he is their Heir and Creator. In relation to God, he is "the effulgence of his glory, and the very image of his substance." There may have been a time when there were no "worlds"; there never was a time when God was without glory, and that glory was ever being revealed through the Son. He is related to the Father as the sun's rays are related to the sun. Furthermore, he is "the very image of his substance," or "express image of his person," or "exact representation of his very being." Both the words "effulgence" and "image" are intended to express and to emphasize the same idea, namely, the perfect revelation of God embodied in Christ.

d. "And upholding all things by the word of his power." He who was before all things, who created all things, who is the Goal or Heir of all things, is further declared to be the Sustainer of all things. He not merely supports, as one might support a weight, but he carries forward, he guides, he governs, he brings to its right conclusion the whole course of nature and of history.

e. "When he had made purification of sins" is a clause which brings the writer to the heart of his message. He is concerned with the fact, not merely or chiefly that Christ is the Revealer of God, but that he is the Redeemer of man. This redemptive work is here defined as making "purification of sins." This high-priestly work of Christ is the great theme of the epistle. As the guilt and consciousness of sin are removed, access to God and fellowship with him are made possible. That such access may be enjoyed and lives of holiness may be lived is the continual aim of the epistle.

f. The finished act of "purification" is followed by exaltation. Christ then "sat down on the right hand of the Majesty on high." The expression must not suggest locality but supreme power. It does not denote any particular place in the universe but indicates that sovereign spiritual influence which Christ exerts as the divine Mediator between God and man.

It is this enthronement which shows the superiority of the Son to the angels, as the writer adds, "Having become by so much better than the angels, as he hath inherited a more excellent name than they." This phrase is really a transition to the argument of the epistle, in which the writer shows the superiority of the Son to angels and to all other mediators between God and men. It forms, however, a fitting conclusion to the verses which precede. They show the supremacy of the Son as the Revealer of God, and also as the Redeemer of men. To accomplish this redemption he himself became a man and in virtue of his redeeming work he has been given a "name," a rank, a dignity above that accorded to the highest of created beings. He is, indeed, the universal King. Those who would know life in all its fullness and all its glory must remain loyal to this divine, incarnate, redeeming, ascended Lord.

2. CHRIST AND THE ANGELS   Chs. 1:5 to 2:18

a. Revealing God   Ch. 1:5-14

> 5 *For unto which of the angels said he at any time,*
> *Thou art my Son,*
> *This day have I begotten thee?*
> *and again,*
> *I will be to him a Father,*
> *And he shall be to me a Son?*
> 6 *And when he again bringeth in the firstborn into the world he saith, And let all the angels of God worship him.*
> 7 *And of the angels he saith,*
> *Who maketh his angels winds,*
> *And his ministers a flame of fire:*
> 8 *but of the Son he saith,*
> *Thy throne, O God, is for ever and ever;*

> *And the sceptre of uprightness is the sceptre of thy king-*
> *dom.*
> 9 *Thou hast loved righteousness, and hated iniquity;*
> *Therefore God, thy God, hath anointed thee*
> *With the oil of gladness above thy fellows.*
> 10 *And,*
> *Thou, Lord, in the beginning didst lay the foundation*
> *of the earth,*
> *And the heavens are the works of thy hands:*
> 11 *They shall perish; but thou continuest:*
> *And they all shall wax old as doth a garment;*
> 12 *And as a mantle shalt thou roll them up,*
> *As a garment, and they shall be changed:*
> *But thou art the same,*
> *And thy years shall not fail.*
> 13 *But of which of the angels hath he said at any time,*
> *Sit thou on my right hand,*
> *Till I make thine enemies the footstool of thy feet?*
> 14 *Are they not all ministering spirits, sent forth to do*
> *service for the sake of them that shall inherit salvation?*

The comparison of Christ with the angels as a mediator between God and men forms the substance of the first two chapters of the epistle. Chapter 1:5-14 represents Christ as the supreme Revelation of God; ch. 2:5-18 represents him as the true Representative of men.

Between these two passages a warning is introduced, intimating the peril of neglecting the offer of salvation which has come through Christ in view of the penalties inflicted upon those who disobeyed the message which came through angels. (Vs. 1-4.) What then are angels? Are they mere creatures of fancy, as fairies and gnomes and elves? Is the word only a figure of speech which personifies the forces of nature and denotes winds or fire or storm? Or does the term describe the spirits of those who have survived death and constitute the inhabitants of the unseen world?

Possibly no more helpful answer can be given than that of the author of Hebrews: "Are they not all ministering

(Hebrews 1:14)

I. They are actual beings.
   A. Of surpassing power & intelligence
   B. Serve God by their ministry to the people of God

II. They are not divine.

III. They are not to be worshipped.

IV. They are distinct from human beings those in heaven as well as those on earth

V. Man is "a little lower than the angels," yet the redeemed are to someday "judge angels."

spirits, sent forth to do service for the sake of them that shall inherit salvation?" Accordingly it must be concluded that they are actual beings, of surpassing power and intelligence, whose special task it is to serve God by their ministry to the people of God. Thus they are not divine. They are not to be worshiped. They are distinct from human beings who are living on earth or in heaven. Such seems to be the representation of Scripture. Men have been created "a little lower than the angels," yet in the world to come the redeemed are to "judge angels."

In the Old Testament narrative there were frequent references to these messengers of God, and in the gospel story they are specially prominent in the scenes of the nativity and of the passion and ascension of Christ. They appear also in the early history of the church.

Aside from the statement of Scripture nothing is known of these mysterious beings. It is unwise to reject these statements as embodying ancient superstitions, and equally unwise to allow the fancy to play upon them with too great freedom.

In the mind of the writer angels were venerated because of their part in the giving of the Law to Israel. (Acts 7:53; Gal. 3:19.) For this reason he begins his argument by proving the superiority of Christ to angels. Such proof might seem superfluous. If Christ was divine why need he be compared with any created beings? It is because the writer is concerned with the work of mediating between God and men. Even a divine mediator might not be a perfect mediator. Yet one who was both divine and human would thus be perfect. For this reason the writer proceeds to show that Christ is superior to the greatest of all mediators, namely, the angels. He is superior because, as the Son of God, he is the supreme manifestation of God.

The writer of the epistle proves this superiority by the quotation of seven Old Testament passages. Six of these are from The Psalms and one is from The Second Book of Samuel. By way of contrast with the angels, Christ is declared to be a Son while they are servants; he is Sovereign while they are subjects; he is Creator while they are creatures; he is Heir of all things while they are ministers to those who are to inherit his salvation and to share his glory.

Sonship

(1)

The writer has already stated (v. 4) that by his exaltation to the right hand of God, Christ had been given a higher dignity than that of the angels. In accordance with that dignity he had been assigned the title of Son, a title which God did not apply to angels. The quotation is taken from Ps. 2:7:

> "Thou art my Son,
> This day have I begotten thee."

The psalmist had reference, first of all, to the coronation of some earthly king; but the author of Hebrews, as was commonly done in interpreting Hebrew poetry, saw in the words a prediction of the Messiah. "This day" referred to the time when the king entered upon his exalted office. In the case of Christ, Paul interpreted the "day" as defining the time of his resurrection. (Acts 13:33.) When he rose from the dead and ascended into heaven and "sat down on the right hand of the Majesty on high," then, in a sense never true of angels, he was declared to be the Son of God.

Guidance

(2)

The second quotation, from II Sam. 7:14, contains words spoken by Nathan in reference to the heirs of David, who are assured of divine grace and guidance for their kingly tasks. These words are taken as finding their real fulfillment in Christ and not in angels:

> "I will be to him a Father,
> And he shall be to me a Son."

Prophecy

(3)

The next quotation, from Deut. 32:43 (LXX) and Ps. 97:7, is interpreted as a prophecy, not of resurrection or incarnation, but of the Second Advent of Christ, when he is to appear "in the glory of his Father with the holy angels" but far superior to the angels: "And when he again bringeth in the firstborn into the world he saith, And let all the angels of God worship him."

In contrast with this homage to be paid to the Son by the angels, the latter are described as servants, merely dependent and perishable, like the forces of nature. This quotation is based on Ps. 104:4:

Permanent

> "Who maketh his angels winds,
> And his ministers a flame of fire."

In further contrast with these "ministering spirits," the Son is declared to be a divine Sovereign whose rule is eternal. This rule is, furthermore, a righteous rule, exercised also with unique joy. (See Ps. 45:6-7.)

Divine

5

> "Thy throne, O God, is for ever and ever;
> And the sceptre of uprightness is the sceptre of thy kingdom.
> Thou hast loved righteousness, and hated iniquity;
> Therefore God, thy God, hath anointed thee
> With the oil of gladness above thy fellows."

The Son is furthermore designated, in the quotation from Ps. 102:25-27, as the eternal Creator in contrast with the angels whom he brought into being:

Creator

> "Thou, Lord, in the beginning didst lay the foundation of the earth,
> And the heavens are the works of thy hands:
> They shall perish; but thou continuest:
> And they all shall wax old as doth a garment;
> And as a mantle shalt thou roll them up,
> As a garment, and they shall be changed:
> But thou art the same,
> And thy years shall not fail."

The last contrast is linked with the first (Heb. 1:5) by the clause with which it is introduced: "But of which of the angels hath he said at any time." In the former case the thought was of the greater "name" given to the Son;

Position

(7)

here it is of his superior place and power, as indicated by a quotation from Ps. 110:1, a Messianic Psalm:

"Sit thou on my right hand,
Till I make thine enemies the footstool of thy feet."

This figure of speech is borrowed from an ancient custom followed by Joshua when he commanded his captains of war to place their feet upon the necks of the conquered kings. Here it is used to picture the ultimate universal reign of Christ. His perfected Kingdom is the goal toward which all human history moves. He is now seated "on the right hand of the Majesty on high"; he is yet to wield the scepter of dominion over all his foes. No such rule is exercised by angels. Whatever their rank, they are all assigned the humble task of "ministering spirits, sent forth to do service for the sake of them that shall inherit salvation." The word "salvation" is used in the New Testament to denote an experience which is past and present and future. In one sense believers have been saved; in another they are being saved; and in a third sense they are to be saved. Salvation is deliverance from the guilt and penalty of sin, from the power of sin, and finally from the presence of sin. As the perfected Kingdom of Christ is still in the future, so, too, is the complete salvation of those who belong to him and are to share his glory. They are yet to enter upon their full privileges; they are to "inherit salvation." Meanwhile, as they put their trust in their exalted Lord, and look to him for needed grace, they are comforted and sustained in their struggles and their tears by the knowledge that unseen messengers are ministering to their needs and guarding them on their journey toward the city of the great King.

Present Tense, Greek

b. A Warning Against Neglect   Ch. 2:1-4

1 *Therefore we ought to give the more earnest heed to the things that were heard, lest haply we drift away* from

them. *2 For if the word spoken through angels proved stedfast, and every transgression and disobedience received a just recompense of reward; 3 how shall we escape, if we neglect so great a salvation? which having at the first been spoken through the Lord, was confirmed unto us by them that heard; 4 God also bearing witness with them, both by signs and wonders, and by manifold powers, and by gifts of the Holy Spirit, according to his own will.*

It is the method of this writer to the Hebrews to use the truth which he has established as the basis for an exhortation or warning which he addresses to his readers. These warnings may seem to interrupt his argument. In a certain measure this is true. They are somewhat of the nature of parentheses. However, they touch the very heart of the epistle, as they are all designed to keep the readers true to Christ and to prevent their becoming apostate from the faith.

The first of these warnings is against indifference to the saving message spoken by Christ, and it is summed up in the words, "How shall we escape, if we neglect so great a salvation?"

The writer has just demonstrated the superiority of Christ to the angels, as the perfect and final Revelation of God to men. On this fact he bases the warning that neglect of the salvation proclaimed by Christ, and attested by his followers and also by miracles and by gifts of the Holy Spirit, will merit more severe penalties than were inflicted upon those who disobeyed the law spoken by angels. It is to be noted that the appeal is addressed to Christians. "Therefore we ought to give the more earnest heed to the things that were heard," is the warning. The need is not that of a new revelation, a new message, a new religion. God has spoken. His Son is the supreme, final, sufficient Message to men. The need is that of a fuller knowledge of Christ and of a more earnest attention to the revelation in Christ. It is a fuller appreciation of the riches of grace in Christ, for which this author continually pleads.

If there is no actual advance in knowledge, or if there is indifference and disregard, then believers stand in imminent peril: "We ought to [we must] give the more earnest heed . . . lest haply we drift away." That is the danger. The figure is that of a ship drifting from its moorings. More literally the word means "to be carried past," or to be swept along past the sure anchorage afforded by the gospel of Christ. To such peril all Christians are exposed. The currents of adverse thought and action are so continuous and so strong that earnestness, devotion, and resolution are demanded in case believers are not to be swept away from their Christian convictions and confession and hopes.

Nor is the danger merely that of losing what has been bestowed and enjoyed; it is the danger of severe penalties. The argument is from the less to the greater. "If the word spoken through angels proved stedfast, and every transgression and disobedience received a just recompense of reward; how shall we escape, if we neglect so great a salvation?" The "word spoken through angels" denotes the Mosaic law. That angels were the mediators in the giving of this law is indicated in Deut. 33:2; Ps. 68:17; Acts 7:53; Gal. 3:19. The reasoning is that if this revelation, introduced by angels, was so sacred that all disobedience to it was severely punished, with still greater rigor will those be treated who are indifferent to the clearer and fuller revelation in Christ, who has been shown to be "so much better than the angels."

This perfect and final revelation, this salvation mediated by Christ, is shown to be "great" in at least three particulars: first of all, in its original proclamation; second, in its secure transmission; third, in its divine attestation. It was proclaimed first by the Lord Jesus Christ himself. No angel was the messenger, but the Son of God, who now is seated "on the right hand of the Majesty on high." His supreme exaltation and divine glory indicate the truthfulness of the message he delivered in the days of his earthly ministry.

Nor has the message been corrupted. It has been

"confirmed unto us by them that heard" him. By their words, and by the experience of their own lives, the immediate disciples of the Lord transmitted to the writer and his fellow believers the exact content of the saving truth they had received from the Lord.

Still further was the gospel message attested by God himself, as the writer declares, "God also bearing witness with them, both by signs and wonders, and by manifold powers, and by gifts of the Holy Spirit, according to his own will." The words translated "signs," "wonders," and "powers" might be applied to any or all of those manifestations usually called "miracles." "Signs" indicates their design of attesting a divine revelation and teaching some spiritual truth; "wonders" expresses their effect upon the observers; "powers" denotes the exercise of divine energy and points to God as their source.

In addition to the attestation of the gospel message "gifts of the Holy Spirit" were granted particularly to members of the apostolic church. These were known as "χαρίσματα," or "spiritual gifts," and included the gifts of healing, of prophecy, and of "tongues." All were specially designed to authenticate the truth revealed in Christ.

It is not want of evidence that turns one from the Christian faith; nor can it be the discovery that Christianity lacks foundation in historic fact. Apostasy is caused by the failure to face evidence and by indifference to a divinely attested gospel. If we are not to drift away from our Christian convictions, we must give earnest heed to the things which we have heard. We must more fully appreciate and more constantly appropriate in personal experience the message of salvation which was first "spoken through the Lord."

c. Representing Man   Ch. 2:5-18

5 For not unto angels did he subject the world to come, whereof we speak. 6 But one hath somewhere testified, saying,
What is man, that thou art mindful of him?

Or the son of man, that thou visitest him?
7 *Thou madest him a little lower than the angels;*
   Thou crownedst him with glory and honor,
   And didst set him over the works of thy hands:
8 *Thou didst put all things in subjection under his feet.*
For in that he subjected all things unto him, he left nothing that is not subject to him. But now we see not yet all things subjected to him. 9 But we behold him who hath been made a little lower than the angels, even Jesus, because of the suffering of death crowned with glory and honor, that by the grace of God he should taste of death for every man. 10 For it became him, for whom are all things, and through whom are all things, in bringing many sons unto glory, to make the author of their salvation perfect through sufferings. 11 For both he that sanctifieth and they that are sanctified are all of one: for which cause he is not ashamed to call them brethren, 12 saying,

   I will declare thy name unto my brethren,
   In the midst of the congregation will I sing thy praise.
13 *And again, I will put my trust in him. And again, Behold, I and the children whom God hath given me. 14 Since then the children are sharers in flesh and blood, he also himself in like manner partook of the same; that through death he might bring to nought him that had the power of death, that is, the devil; 15 and might deliver all them who through fear of death were all their lifetime subject to bondage. 16 For verily not to angels doth he give help, but he giveth help to the seed of Abraham. 17 Wherefore it behooved him in all things to be made like unto his brethren, that he might become a merciful and faithful high priest in things pertaining to God, to make propitiation for the sins of the people. 18 For in that he himself hath suffered being tempted, he is able to succor them that are tempted.*

In the first chapter of the epistle its author has shown the superiority of Christ to angels as being the perfect manifestation of God; he now proceeds to show his superiority in his being the ideal representative of man. He argues that the universal sovereignty promised to man has been attained only by Christ, and this by way of incarnation and necessary suffering. Of the return of Christ in majesty and triumph the author has already spoken. (Ch. 1:6.) Christ's righteous and blessed reign is yet to be universal. Such sovereignty over the coming age of glory has not been promised to angels: "For not unto angels did he subject the world to come, whereof we speak." The promise has been made to Christ and to those who follow him. It is contained in Psalm 8. Here is found a statement of the weakness and insignificance of man, and of his inferiority to the angels; but here is also an assurance of man's dominion and universal rule.

"But one hath somewhere testified, saying,
"What is man, that thou art mindful of him?
Or the son of man, that thou visitest him?
Thou madest him a little lower than the angels;
Thou crownedst him with glory and honor,
And didst set him over the works of thy hands:
Thou didst put all things in subjection under
his feet."

The language is very strong. The promised sovereignty extends to "all things"; as the writer insists, "For in that he subjected all things unto him, he left nothing that is not subject to him."

Now man is not seen exercising any such universal dominion: "But now we see not yet all things subjected to him." However, in Christ we see realized both the humiliation and the exaltation of which the psalmist wrote —the former by his incarnation and death, the latter by his glorification and by his sovereignty in the coming age when his Kingdom is to be perfected. As the writer declares, "But we behold him who hath been made a little lower than the angels, even Jesus, because of the suffering of death crowned with glory and honor, that by the grace of God he should taste of death for every man." It is natural that the name of Jesus should be used here, for it was his human title and reminds one of his humiliation and suffering. The mystery of his suffering and death the writer does not explain. He declares that it was by the grace of God, that the Father allowed his Son to suffer for the redemption of sinful man.

This suffering was a divine necessity. It was in accordance with the nature of God. It was part of a gracious purpose for the salvation of men. "It became him, for whom are all things, and through whom are all things," him who is the reason and the cause of all things, "in bringing many sons unto glory, to make the author of their salvation perfect through sufferings." The word translated "author" denotes origin or source, yet it also has the implication of "pioneer." Christ is not only the author of salvation; he is also the leader who goes before the saved, treading the same path. By treading that path he was made "perfect." This does not mean that he needed to be cleansed from any moral fault, but that by his sufferings he became perfect as a Savior, with that complete spiritual development and that ability to sympathize and to deliver which could be possible only to one who had experienced as a man temptation and pain and death. Thus the "glory" to which he was enabled to bring his followers was to include an ultimate triumph over all these foes by which men are terrified and enslaved.

His followers are here called "sons," and sons of "him, for whom are all things, and through whom are all things," that is to say, "sons of God." This does not mean that they partake of the divine attributes of him who is in a unique sense the Son of God, but that they are to partake in his triumph over sin and death and are to share his dignity and destiny, even as he shared with them the experiences of suffering. They, therefore, are his brethren, sons of one Father: "For both he that sanctifieth and they that are sanctified are all of one."

This relationship Christ does not hesitate to admit: "He is not ashamed to call them brethren." Since he and those whom he saves have God as their common Father, he addresses them as brothers, expressing with them his trustful dependence upon God, and naming himself the Elder Brother in the family of the redeemed. To show the willingness of Christ to take his place among men as their brother, the writer quotes two passages from the Old Testament as though they had been spoken by Christ (Ps. 22:22 and Isa. 8:17-18):

"I will declare thy name unto my brethren,
   In the midst of the congregation will I sing thy praise";

"I will put my trust in him. . . . Behold, I and the children whom God hath given me."

The first of these quotations is from a psalm which Christ applied to himself when on the cross. The significant words in the first line are "my brethren." The import of the second line is that Christ is represented as partaking with his brethren in the praise of God.

The passage from Isaiah shows, first, Christ's brotherhood with men in his confessed dependence upon God; and, second, his close, conscious association with his fellows, the children of God, who are committed to his care.

To experience this brotherhood with men, it was necessary for Christ to become a man, and to submit to all the weakness and temptations common to the lot of man, even to death itself; yet this was in order that he might deliver men from their bondage to sin and to death. In the words of the author, "Since then the children are sharers in flesh and blood, he also himself in like manner partook of the same; that through death he might bring to nought him that had the power of death, that is, the devil; and might deliver all them who through fear of death were all their lifetime subject to bondage."

That Christ partook of flesh and blood does not mean merely that he assumed a physical body, but that he entered upon human life with all its struggles, its perils, and its pain. His chief adversary is described as "the devil," whose dread weapon of death kept mankind under a perpetual bondage of fear. That the devil "had the power of death" does not mean that he could determine the continuance or the ending of human life. It probably refers to the part played by the tempter in bringing sin into the world, with its dire penalty of death, and to his ability thus to give to death its most terrifying aspect as "the wages of sin." However, Christ by his victory over sin and death has been able to "bring to nought" this enemy of men and to overcome the fear of death. Not that this double victory is yet complete. The devil is not powerless, and Christians naturally regard with revulsion the anguish of body, the distress and sorrow, which usually accompany "the last enemy" of mankind. However, the victory of Christ was real. Christians can share his triumph in their conflict with the defeated foe; and, as to death, Christians can regard it as a servant in dark livery who ushers them into a larger and a better life. Then, too, there is something prophetic in the words. They point forward to the perfected Kingdom of Christ and to that "glory" which the sons of God shall yet attain, when death shall have been destroyed, and they shall have been delivered from the bondage of fear and shall have entered upon their destiny of universal rule.

Thus it is that the sufferings of Christ were necessary if he was to redeem man. "For verily," continues the writer, "not to angels doth he give help, but he giveth help to the seed of Abraham." He did not "lay hold of to deliver" a heavenly host of sinless and deathless beings, but of sinful and mortal men, whom the writer designates as "the seed of Abraham," apparently first having in mind the people of his own race.

"Wherefore it behooved him in all things to be made like unto his brethren." It was absolutely necessary that he must become a man and suffer like men if he was to accomplish his saving work. This work the writer now describes in terms not of a deliverance but of a priestly service: "That he might become a merciful and faithful high priest in things pertaining to God, to make propitiation for the sins of the people." Here the very essence of the message is reached, for the whole epistle is written to set forth the high priesthood of Christ. His office is that of making an atonement. He removes the obstacles that sin has erected, so that it is possible for his people to enjoy free and unrestricted access to God. This he is able to do in view of his experiences of human suffering and trial. These experiences fit him to be "merciful and faithful" in all those acts in which he mediates between men and God. "For in that he himself hath suffered being tempted, he is able to succor them that are tempted." Thus the fact that Christ for a time was made "a little lower than the angels" is no evidence against his being superior to the angels, for by incarnation and suffering and death he was qualified to render for man a ministry even higher than that assigned to angels. He became able to sympathize and to save, and is destined to be, as the Representative of man, the universal Sovereign in "the world to come."

3. CHRIST AND MOSES   CHS. 3; 4

a. The Son and the Servant   Ch. 3:1-6

1 Wherefore, holy brethren, partakers of a heavenly calling, consider the Apostle and High Priest of our confession, even Jesus; 2 who was faithful to him that appointed him, as also was Moses in all his house. 3 For he hath been counted worthy of more glory than Moses, by so much as he that built the house hath more honor than the house. 4 For every house is builded by some one; but he that built all things is God. 5 And Moses indeed was faithful in all his house as a servant, for a testimony of those things which were afterward to be spoken; 6 but Christ as a son, over his house; whose house are we, if we hold fast our boldness and the glorying of our hope firm unto the end.

The writer has shown the superiority of Christ to angels. He now shows that he is superior to Moses. Such a comparison may seem needless. Angels are regarded as beings of supernatural power and glory. If, then, Christ is "so much better than the angels," he obviously must be superior to mortal man. However, it is necessary to remember the reverence in which Moses was held by the writer and his readers. Angels may have been the celestial agents in communicating the law; but Moses was known as the lawgiver, the very embodiment and glory of the divine revelation and of the old dispensation with which Christ is being compared.

Then, too, this contrast is drawn because of the practical purpose of the writer. He is constantly encouraging his readers to be true to Christ. If Moses was faithful in all the household of God, and therefore worthy to be trusted, even though he held the place of a servant, much more is Christ to be trusted who holds in the household of God the position of a son. Furthermore, those who followed Moses into the wilderness turned back and perished because of their unbelief; their pitiful fate becomes, as developed by the writer, a warning to any who may be tempted to forsake Christ and to become apostates from the faith.

The contrast, then, is much the same as in the case of the angels. It is the contrast of a servant with a Son. Angels were ministering spirits, Christ is the sovereign Son of God. Moses was faithful in God's household "as a servant," but Christ "as a son" over the household of God.

In turning to this new comparison, that of Christ with Moses, the writer addresses his readers as "holy brethren, partakers of a heavenly calling." The word translated "holy" means "separated," that is, separated unto the service of God. However, the phrase needs to be understood in its usual New Testament sense of fellow Christians. The "heavenly calling" may imply a contrast between the earthly promises to the followers of Moses and the hopes of things above shared by the followers of Christ. It is a common contrast in this epistle, the contrast between the world and heaven, between the material and transient and the ideal and eternal.

These "holy brethren" are urged to "consider the Apostle and High Priest of our confession, even Jesus." To "consider" means so to observe as to appreciate and understand. It is a main purpose of the epistle to prevent apostasy by urging the readers to realize the incomparable glory and saving power of Christ. The exhortation is linked to the two preceding chapters by the connecting "wherefore." If God has spoken his final message through his Son, who is his Apostle, and if Christ is "a merciful and faithful high priest" who suffered for men and has been crowned with glory, if he can sympathize and save, then surely we must "consider" him "the Apostle and High Priest of our confession."

The special fact to be considered is the faithfulness, the trustworthiness of our Savior. In this regard he is likened to Moses. He "was faithful to him that appointed him, as also was Moses in all his house." The words "his house" denote "God's house," "his household," "his people," the organized community in which he dwells. In all his relations to this "house" Moses was faithful. The writer in no way disparages Moses. It is almost startling to read, "Jesus . . . was faithful . . . as . . . Moses." Indeed, Moses was faithful. He poured out his life in the service of Israel. He made every sacrifice; he was willing for the sake of the people to be blotted out of the book of God. He was worthy to be trusted.

Much more should Christ be trusted—not because of greater faithfulness, but because of his superior dignity and power: "For he hath been counted worthy of more glory than Moses, by so much as he that built the house hath more honor than the house"; that is, God assigned to his Son the position of one who organizes and regulates a household, while to Moses was given the position of a servant within the household. As in every house there must be some administrator in charge, so it is in God's household. He who "built all things," and who therefore brought his own spiritual family into being, assigned to one and to another their positions and functions. In thus arranging, he made Moses a servant. "And Moses indeed was faithful in all his house," that is, in God's house, as a servant bearing testimony to "those things which were afterward to be spoken," that is, to those truths which were to be more fully revealed through Christ. To Christ, however, was given the authority which belongs to a Son, who is placed in complete control of the household. He was appointed to be "over his house," that is, over God's household.

Of this spiritual family all Christians are members: "Whose house are we." There is, however, a condition: "If we hold fast our boldness and the glorying of our hope firm unto the end." It is the aim of the writer to encourage such loyalty to Christ, such confident expectation of the heavenly inheritance and of perfected fellowship with God. We, then, do well to "consider" him, who, unlike Moses and all other servants, is in the place of supreme power, the Creator and Administrator of God's family, the unique, the sovereign Son.

b. A Warning Against Unbelief   Chs. 3:7 to 4:13

(1) The Example of Israel   Ch. 3:7-19

7   *Wherefore, even as the Holy Spirit saith,*
    To-day if ye shall hear his voice,

8   *Harden not your hearts, as in the provocation,*
    Like as in the day of the trial in the wilderness,

9   *Where your fathers tried me by proving me,*
    And saw my works forty years.

10 *Wherefore I was displeased with this generation,*
    And said, They do always err in their heart:
    But they did not know my ways;

11 *As I sware in my wrath,*

They shall not enter into my rest.
12 Take heed, brethren, lest haply there shall be in any one of you an evil heart of unbelief, in falling away from the living God: 13 but exhort one another day by day, so long as it is called To-day; lest any one of you be hardened by the deceitfulness of sin: 14 for we are become partakers of Christ, if we hold fast the beginning of our confidence firm unto the end: 15 while it is said,

To-day if ye shall hear his voice,
Harden not your hearts, as in the provocation.
16 For who, when they heard, did provoke? nay, did not all they that came out of Egypt by Moses? 17 And with whom was he displeased forty years? was it not with them that sinned, whose bodies fell in the wilderness? 18 And to whom sware he that they should not enter into his rest, but to them that were disobedient? 19 And we see that they were not able to enter in because of unbelief.

In order to encourage loyalty to Christ, the writer has shown the superiority of Christ to Moses. The great lawgiver, deliverer, and leader accomplished with the absolute fidelity his great task for Israel; but to Christ has been accorded a far higher dignity and position as the Son of God, supreme in the household of God.

The mention of Moses, however, gives the writer an opportunity to voice a solemn warning. He cites the tragic example of the disaster which befell the followers of Moses. It was no lack of faithfulness on the part of the great emancipator but entirely a lack of faith on the part of the people that caused them to turn back from the very border of the Land of Promise and to perish in the wilderness. So it will not be because of any want of trustworthiness on the part of Christ but because of "an evil heart of unbelief," if any follower of Christ turns away from him and fails to enter upon the rest that remains for the people of God. The warning, therefore, falls into two parts: the one points out the peril of unbelief; the other, the danger of losing the promised rest.

The former is embodied in a quotation from Psalm 95.

This quotation is introduced by the noteworthy clause, "Even as the Holy Spirit saith," a clause which calls to mind the fact that the writer of this epistle, in making continual reference to the books of the Old Testament, usually attributes them, not to their human authors, but to God as their Source. The psalmist was making a plea for obedience to the voice of God, a plea enforced by a reference to the unbelief of Israel during the wilderness wanderings and the consequent decree of God that they should not be allowed to enter the promised rest in the Land of Canaan:

> "To-day if ye shall hear his voice,
> Harden not your hearts, as in the provocation,
> Like as in the day of the trial in the wilderness,
> Where your fathers tried me by proving me,
> And saw my works forty years.
> Wherefore I was displeased with this generation,
> And said, They do always err in their heart:
> But they did not know my ways;
> As I sware in my wrath,
> They shall not enter into my rest."

This solemn warning the writer to the Hebrews at once applies to his readers: "Take heed, brethren, lest haply there shall be in any one of you an evil heart of unbelief, in falling away from the living God." Unbelief is due to a hardened heart, and hardening of the heart is caused by sin. The result is apostasy. The writer indicates that unfaithfulness to Christ is equivalent to falling away from God. To prevent such a dire issue, the readers are urged to "exhort one another day by day, so long as it is called To-day," that is, to encourage and admonish one another as Christian brethren so long as an opportunity is given to hear the voice of God as he speaks through Christ. Otherwise, unless there is earnest heed and mutual exhortation, they may be hardened through the deceitfulness of sin, for sin in the heart or life blinds people to the real blessedness of the Christian life. It seduces the soul to be disloyal to Christ. Against such peril we must be on our guard: "For we are become partakers of Christ" —we enjoy blessed fellowship with him—"if we hold fast the beginning of our confidence firm unto the end." Continued trust will assure continued fellowship with him, until at last that fellowship shall be complete when he appears and "we shall see him even as he is."

The readers then must heed the solemn warning voiced by the psalmist, as he is heard to say,

> "To-day if ye shall hear his voice,
> Harden not your hearts, as in the provocation."

Christians must not repeat the sinful unfaithfulness of which the Israelites were guilty in the wilderness. But how general was this disobedience on the part of God's ancient people? "For who, when they heard, did provoke? nay, did not all they that came out of Egypt by Moses?" The writer is not concerned with mentioning the insignificant fraction, Joshua and Caleb, who were faithful. He wishes to recall the tragic fact that the entire generation of Israelites which left Egypt and reached the border of Canaan turned back to die in the desert. It was unbelief that caused them to turn back, and the penalty of their unbelief was death. It was this unbelief and consequent disobedience which displeased God. "With whom was he displeased forty years? was it not with them that sinned, whose bodies fell in the wilderness?" Pathetic indeed is that picture—weary wanderers, homeless and hopeless, falling one by one, doomed to die and to leave their bodies in unmarked graves. Such is the tragedy, the hopelessness, of those who turn away from Christ.

Nor is the picture merely that of the death which awaits; it is the tragedy of what might have been enjoyed—the Land of Promise and the rest of God. From the blessedness they were excluded by unbelief: "And to whom sware he that they should not enter into his rest, but to them that were disobedient? And we see that they were not able to enter in because of unbelief." Thus the unbelief was the cause of the disobedience. They did not trust God to give them strength to overcome the enemies who opposed them and so they refused to go forward and to achieve the conquest which would have been possible by faith. "They were not able to enter in"; unbelief made it impossible. The application to the readers is most obvious. They must not hesitate to go forward. Obstacles and difficulties, opposition and scorn beset their faith, like the walled cities and giants which terrified Israel of old; but nothing must be allowed to make them disloyal to Christ, nothing be regarded as sufficient to exclude them from the Land of Promise, and to turn them back to the wilderness with its misery and its graves.

(2) The Rest That Remains   Ch. 4:1-13

1 Let us fear therefore, lest haply, a promise being left of entering into his rest, any one of you should seem to have come short of it. 2 For indeed we have had good tidings preached unto us, even as also they: but the word of hearing did not profit them, because it was not united by faith with them that heard. 3 For we who have believed do enter into that rest; even as he hath said,

As I sware in my wrath,
They shall not enter into my rest:
although the works were finished from the foundation of the world. 4 For he hath said somewhere of the seventh day on this wise, And God rested on the seventh day from all his works; 5 and in this place again,
They shall not enter into my rest.
6 Seeing therefore it remaineth that some should enter thereinto, and they to whom the good tidings were before preached failed to enter in because of disobedience, 7 he again defineth a certain day, To-day, saying in David so long a time afterward (even as hath been said before),
To-day if ye shall hear his voice,
Harden not your hearts.

8 For if Joshua had given them rest, he would not have spoken afterward of another day. 9 There remaineth therefore a sabbath rest for the people of God. 10 For he that is entered into his rest hath himself also rested from his works, as God did from his. 11 Let us therefore give diligence to enter into that rest, that no man fall after the same example of disobedience. 12 For the word of God is living, and active, and sharper than any two-edged sword, and piercing even to the dividing of soul and spirit, of both joints and marrow, and quick to discern the thoughts and intents of the heart. 13 And there is no creature that is not manifest in his sight: but all things are naked and laid open before the eyes of him with whom we have to do.

What is meant by the "rest" of God? Does it describe a present or a future experience? Opinions differ. Some persons employ the word to describe Christian life in general; and indeed this life well may be regarded as a fulfillment of the precious promise which fell from the lips of Christ: "Come unto me, all ye that labor and are heavy laden, and I will give you rest. Take my yoke upon you, and learn of me; for I am meek and lowly in heart: and ye shall find rest unto your souls."

Others employ the phrase to describe a unique experience attained by some Christians who, by complete surrender to the will of Christ and constant dependence upon the power of Christ, enter upon a state of "perfect peace and rest." The words are thus taken as equivalent to another popular phrase, namely, "The rest of faith."

The write of The Epistle to the Hebrews, however, seems to employ the words to point to the heavenly rest which awaits the followers of Christ; indeed, to a share in the rest into which God himself entered when he had finished all his creative work. The purpose of the writer is to keep his readers from disloyalty to Christ and to encourage them to persevere until they enter upon the blessedness which is to be theirs in the perfected Kingdom of Christ. He has been warning them from the pitiful example of Israel. Because of unbelief the ancient people of God had to turn back from the border of Canaan, and failed to enjoy the peace and privileges and saving fellowship with God which might have been theirs in the Land of Promise. He now warns his readers lest by unbelief they may fail to attain the promised rest which the future contains for the true people of God. "Let us fear therefore," he writes, "lest haply, a promise being left of entering into his rest, any one of you should seem to have come short of it." The author assumes that the promised rest is still available. It is open to faith, but to faith alone. He does not intimate that any of his readers will fail to attain it. The warning is delicately worded; but even any appearance or suspicion of failure is to be avoided.

The promise is to all Christians, quite as truly as the offer of Canaan was made to Israel: "For indeed we have had good tidings preached unto us, even as also they: but the word of hearing did not profit them, because it was not united by faith with them that heard." Christians, then, should not follow this example of unbelief. If they continue in faith they will be sure to enter into the promised rest: "For we who have believed do enter into that rest." It was destined to be enjoyed by the followers of Christ. The Jews of Moses' time were excluded from it, as the psalmist says,

> "As I sware in my wrath,
> They shall not enter into my rest."

Yet even from the Creation of the world the rest had been prepared: "The works were finished from the foundation of the world." That there was a rest of God from the beginning is evident from the statement of Scripture that "God rested on the seventh day from all his works." That there is such a rest remaining is attested by the very statement, "They shall not enter into my rest."

There is, then, a rest of God. Israel failed to attain it

because of unbelief. Yet the very psalm which speaks of
"to-day" as a time of opportunity and warns against
disobedience indicates that the "rest" is still available. Indeed, some are sure to enter in. Or, to quote the words
of the author, "Seeing therefore it remaineth that some
should enter thereinto, and they to whom the good tidings
were before preached failed to enter in because of disobedience, he again defineth a certain day, To-day, saying in
David so long a time afterward (even as hath been said
before),

> "To-day if ye shall hear his voice,
> Harden not your hearts."

The very fact that the psalm was written long after the
people had been led by Joshua into the Land of Promise
indicates that Israel never enjoyed the real rest which had
been promised: "For if Joshua had given them rest, he
[God] would not have spoken afterward of another day."

Thus the conclusion is beyond question: "There remaineth therefore a sabbath rest for the people of God."
Here it is called "a sabbath rest" to identify it with the
rest of God, who is said to have rested on the Sabbath, or
seventh day. It does not denote an experience of actual
inactivity, but marks the completion of a period of labor.
Like the ideal Sabbath Day, it is to be a time of blessed
fellowship with God and of helpful service; but also it is
to be a time when the toils and labors of life are ended.
"For he that is entered into his [God's] rest," continues
the writer, "hath himself also rested from his works, as
God did from his." The words seem to be echoed by John
in his Apocalypse: "They may rest from their labors; for
their works follow with them."

The writer now naturally presses home the lesson drawn
from the Old Testament references: "Let us therefore
give diligence to enter into that rest, that no man fall
after the same example of disobedience." The example
is that of the generation of Israelites which was led to the

very border of Canaan, and then in stubborn unbelief refused to obey the command of God and turned back to
die in the wilderness.

Another reason is added for putting heart and soul into
our religion, and for acting in faith upon the promises of
God and particularly upon the promise of rest. This reason is found in the nature of "the word of God," by which
is meant his revelation in Christ, his offer of grace. When
this comes to a man, with its promises of the highest con-
ceivable good, it searches his inmost desires and motives.
It makes evident whether or not he is really seeking for
purity and holiness and fellowship with God, or whether
lower desires are dominating his soul: "For the word of
God is living, and active, and sharper than any two-edged
sword, and piercing even to the dividing of soul and spirit,
of both joints and marrow, and quick to discern the
thoughts and intents of the heart." Christ is still the Touch-
stone of character; and the offer of salvation through faith
in Christ penetrates into the deepest recesses of a man's
being and discovers the hidden secrets of the heart.

Nor is it merely the message and promises of God which
are thus living and effective. We are responsible to a
living God whose all-seeing eye none can escape. He
knows perfectly all our disobedience and unbelief, yet he
is ready to grant all needed grace as we draw near to him
in the name of Christ: "There is no creature that is not
manifest in his sight: but all things are naked and laid
open before the eyes of him with whom we have to do."

c. The Ascended High Priest   Ch. 4:14-16

*14 Having then a great high priest, who hath passed
through the heavens, Jesus the Son of God, let us hold fast
our confession. 15 For we have not a high priest that
cannot be touched with the feeling of our infirmities; but
one that hath been in all points tempted like as we are, yet
without sin. 16 Let us therefore draw near with boldness
unto the throne of grace, that we may receive mercy, and
may find grace to help us in time of need.*

In a superb paragraph of exhortation and encouragement, the writer concludes his comparison of Christ and Moses. He also touches the very heart of his doctrinal discussion by presenting Christ as "a great high priest," and thus introduces the next step in the discussion, wherein Christ is shown to be greater than Aaron.

That there is a connection with the thought of the previous paragraph is evident, although indeed the figure of speech is suddenly changed. There the thought was centered upon Moses, the great deliverer and leader of Israel, and it was shown that neither Moses nor his followers entered the Land of Promise. Here our Savior is pictured not as a leader but as a high priest, who has "passed through the heavens" into the very presence of God and is able to bring his followers into immediate fellowship with God. Looking back upon the disobedience and failure of Israel, the author therefore encourages his readers to be loyal to Christ: "Having then a great high priest, who hath passed through the heavens, Jesus the Son of God, let us hold fast our confession."

Earlier in the epistle, Christ has been designated as a high priest. Here the adjective "great" is added. Probably this is by way of contrast with the Jewish high priest. Christ has not passed beyond any mere material veil into "a holy place made with hands," but he has penetrated to the very throne of God, and occupies a place of supreme power. His greatness is further indicated by his titles, "Jesus the Son of God." "Jesus" was his human name, indicating his perfect sympathy with men. "The Son of God" indicated his divine dignity and his qualification to mediate between God and men.

The human sympathy of this great High Priest is mentioned as a special encouragement to loyalty. It enforces the exhortation, "Let us hold fast our confession." It is expressed both negatively and positively: "We have not a high priest that cannot be touched with the feeling of our infirmities; but one that hath been in all points tempted like as we are, yet without sin." Christ is able to sympa-

thize with the weaknesses which make it difficult for us
to resist evil, because he himself has suffered the full force
and bitterness of temptation. His conflict with the adversary was no sham battle. His suffering from the allurements of sin and from the bitterness of pain was real and
cruel. In no respect did the temptations of Christ differ
from our own, except in one—they were always overcome.
He remained "without sin."

There are those who believe that the phrase, "Without
sin," means that the one difference lay in the fact that in
the case of Christ temptation never sprang from sinful
desire or was strengthened by the impulses of an evil nature. This is true of his temptations; but it is rather beside
the point, and is an unnecessary refinement. It was the
purpose of the writer to express the victory of Christ over
all temptations, rather than to distinguish between different
kinds of temptation. He wished to encourage his readers
to believe that as Christ had always overcome, so He
could ensure victory to all who would put their trust in him.
Thus he adds, "Let us therefore draw near with boldness
unto the throne of grace, that we may receive mercy, and
may find grace to help us in time of need."

It is because we know our High Priest to be sympathetic
and victorious that we can draw near to him in resolute
confidence. His throne is the seat of divine and omnipo-
tent power, and it is the source from which boundless
grace is bestowed. We draw near to that throne to obtain
mercy, for we are conscious of our sin; we draw near to receive grace, for we confess our weakness. Nor shall we
ever be disappointed as we put our confident trust in our
sympathetic Savior, our victorious and ascended High
Priest.

4. CHRIST AND AARON   Chs. 5 to 7

a. The Qualifications of the High Priest   Ch. 5:1-10

*1 For every high priest, being taken from among men,
is appointed for men in things pertaining to God, that he*

may offer both gifts and sacrifices for sins: 2 who can bear gently with the ignorant and erring, for that he himself also is compassed with infirmity; 3 and by reason thereof is bound, as for the people, so also for himself, to offer for sins. 4 And no man taketh the honor unto himself, but when he is called of God, even as was Aaron. 5 So Christ also glorified not himself to be made a high priest, but he that spake unto him,

Thou art my Son,
This day have I begotten thee:
6 as he saith also in another place,
Thou art a priest for ever
After the order of Melchizedek.

7 Who in the days of his flesh, having offered up prayers and supplications with strong crying and tears unto him that was able to save him from death, and having been heard for his godly fear, 8 though he was a Son, yet learned obedience by the things which he suffered; 9 and having been made perfect, he became unto all them that obey him the author of eternal salvation; 10 named of God a high priest after the order of Melchizedek.

Christ has been shown to be superior to angels, the mediators of the law, and superior to Moses, the deliver, who led the people to the Promised Land. He is now shown to be superior to Aaron, who as the typical high priest was the very symbol and embodiment of the ancient liturgy. He is like Aaron in the priestly nature of his office and in the qualifications for his task. (Ch. 5:1-10.) He is superior to Aaron in that his priesthood is eternal. (Ch. 7.)

In the earlier portions of the epistle, the author has referred to the saving work of Christ under the figure of priestly service; but this extended comparison with Aaron, the first and most famous high priest of Israel, brings the epistle to its very climax in presenting Christ as the great High Priest, and in setting forth the abiding efficacy of his atoning work.

In the opening sentence of his letter the author has referred to Christ as having "made purification of sins." In

comparing Christ with angels he has described him as
having "become a merciful and faithful high priest in
things pertaining to God, to make propitiation for the
sins of the people." In beginning the comparison with
Moses he has appealed to his readers to "consider the
Apostle and High Priest of our confession, even Jesus,"
and in closing the comparison has exhorted them to "draw
near with boldness unto the throne of grace," since we
have "a great high priest, who hath passed through the
heavens," one indeed who can "be touched with the feeling of our infirmities."

With this encouraging exhortation the author introduces
his description of the office and the qualifications of the
high priest: "For every high priest, being taken from
among men, is appointed for men in things pertaining to
God, that he may offer both gifts and sacrifices for sins."
That is to say, our consciousness of sin must not prevent
us from coming with boldness to the throne of grace, for
it is the very office of a high priest to make atonement for
sins. He is appointed of God for this very purpose, and
he fulfills his task with sympathy because he is mindful of
his own weakness. He "can bear gently with the ignorant
and erring, for that he himself also is compassed with infirmity; and by reason thereof is bound, as for the people,
so also for himself, to offer for sins. And no man taketh
the honor unto himself, but when he is called of God, even
as was Aaron."

Thus the author defines the office of high priest, and
states the two supreme qualifications for the office, namely,
human sympathy and divine appointment. Thus, too, he
introduces the name of Aaron, with whose priestly service
he is to compare the atoning work of Christ. He proceeds
then to show how the two qualifications for the office, or,
as he says, for the "the honor," are fulfilled by Christ. He
deals with them, however, in the reverse order: first the
appointment by God, and then the sympathy with men.

The divine appointment is established by two quota-

tions from Scripture: "So Christ also glorified not himself
to be made a high priest, but he that spake unto him,

> "Thou art my Son,
> This day have I begotten thee:

as he saith also in another place,

> Thou art a priest for ever
> After the order of Melchizedek."

The former of these references (Ps. 2:7) has previously
been quoted by the author (Heb. 1:5). It attributes the
Messianic dignity of the Son to a divine decree. The glory
of the risen and exalted Christ finds its source in the will
and purpose of God. The reference makes no mention of
priesthood. Yet the priestly work of Christ is included in
his experience as Son and Savior and universal Sovereign.
The comprehensive dignity of Sonship, including his atoning work, was not of his own seeking, but of divine ordination.

The second reference (Ps. 110:4) specifically designates Christ as "a priest," and adds the significant phrases,
"For ever," and "After the order of Melchizedek." His
priesthood was to be royal and perpetual, of the rank of
Melchizedek. In this regard it was to surpass in dignity
the priesthood of Aaron. The superiority of Christ to
Aaron is further developed in the seventh chapter of the
epistle.

Here, however, the author proceeds to show how Christ,
like Aaron, fulfilled the second condition of being a true
high priest, namely, by his human sympathy.

This qualification has been noted previously by the author. (Heb. 2:18; 4:15.) It is here set forth in the most
vivid phrases. They transport the reader to the shadows
of Gethsemane and to the mysterious darkness of Cal-
vary. "Who in the days of his flesh," says the author, referring, of course, not to Melchizedek but to Christ, "having offered up prayers and supplications with strong crying

and tears unto him that was able to save him from death, and having been heard for his godly fear, though he was a Son, yet learned obedience by the things which he suffered." We see the Savior bowed in agony beneath the olive trees in the Garden. We behold the bloody sweat, and we hear the cry for deliverance. Yet we also witness the victory. We see him come forth submissive to the Father's will, "content with death and shame," fearlessly facing the cross. He "learned obedience by the things which he suffered." He had never been disobedient; but he discovered by painful experience all that obedience and submission may mean. Even when the bitter cup was offered him he was able to say, "Not my will, but thine, be done." He shrank from the cup with all its bitter ingredients, as he was asked to "taste of death for every man." Yet, even though he was the divine Son of God, he submitted to pain and death in accomplishing the will of God. He prayed for deliverance; and he was heard, because of "his godly fear," his submissive trust. The answer came, not in the sense that the cup was removed, but in the sense that by drinking the cup he accomplished the saving purpose of God. He knew that God had the power to deliver him from death; it was the most bitter ingredient of the cup that this power should not be exercised in his behalf. Yet "his godly fear" enabled him to drink the contents of the cup to its very dregs. Surely One who so suffered can sympathize with suffering men. He can do more. He can save: "Having been made perfect, he became unto all them that obey him the author of eternal salvation."

His suffering resulted in moral perfection. It enabled him, like Aaron, to fulfill the qualification of human sympathy. Yet, unlike Aaron, he was not merely a High Priest, but "the author of eternal salvation." The recipients of this salvation are those who "obey him"— not those who profess their faith, not those who are orthodox in their beliefs, not those who are enrolled as church members, but those who consistently, continually, submissively do the will of Christ.

The salvation he provides is "eternal." This is implied in the fact that he has been "named of God a high priest after the order of Melchizedek." Unlike Aaron, Melchizedek held a perpetual priesthood. So the work of Christ is of abiding efficacy. "He is able to save to the uttermost them that draw near unto God through him, seeing he ever liveth to make intercession for them."

b. A Warning Against Falling Away Chs. 5:11 to 6:20

(1) The Readers' Immaturity Ch. 5:11-14

11 Of whom we have many things to say, and hard of interpretation, seeing ye are become dull of hearing. 12 For when by reason of the time ye ought to be teachers, ye have need again that some one teach you the rudiments of the first principles of the oracles of God; and are become such as have need of milk, and not of solid food. 13 For every one that partaketh of milk is without experience of the word of righteousness; for he is a babe. 14 But solid food is for fullgrown men, even those who by reason of use have their senses exercised to discern good and evil.

One who fails to make progress in Christian knowledge thereby places his soul in imminent peril. Such is the solemn consideration in the mind of the writer as he interrupts his argument by an extended warning against apostasy. (Chs. 5:11 to 6:20.)

The digression is due to the fear on the part of the writer that the teaching he is about to give may be too difficult for his readers to understand. He seeks to arouse their attention by rebuking them for their infantile inability to comprehend spiritual truth (ch. 5:11-14), and by a solemn warning against their consequent danger of falling away from Christ (ch. 6:1-8). He then urges them to hold firm their Christian hope, encouraged by their past experience and by the unfailing promise of God. (Vs. 9-20.)

As to the infantile state of the readers, the author is saying in effect: "It is difficult to explain to you the priestly office of Christ because of your immaturity in Christian knowledge. For while you have been Christians long enough to have become instructors of others, you need yourselves to be instructed in the very rudiments of the Christian faith. You are mere infants in your knowledge of the gospel, for one who can understand only the simplest elements of Christian truth is but a babe. The deeper mysteries of the faith can be received only by the mature Christian who is trained to discriminate between what is true and false in religious instruction." (Ch. 5:11-14.)

The theme which the writer is eager yet hesitant to discuss is that of the high priesthood of Christ. "Of whom we have many things to say" (v. 11) might refer to Melchizedek, whose name immediately precedes this phrase and with whose name the writer renews his discussion (ch. 7:1), after the long parenthetic warning (chs. 5:11 to 6:20) which here begins. However, the "of whom" more probably refers to Christ, but to Christ as "a high priest after the order of Melchizedek." It is this royal, universal, eternal priesthood which the writer desires to unfold, a priesthood superior to that of Aaron, superseding that of all other priests and saviors and mediators, and bringing the followers into immediate fellowship with God.

Such a subject was indeed "hard of interpretation." It was not easy to explain, yet the difficulty lay not in the mystery and the glory of the theme, but in the spiritual incapacity of the readers, whom the author describes as having "become dull of hearing." They had lost their spiritual insight, their ability to receive Christian teaching, their sensitiveness to revealed truth.

They should have been advanced in knowledge. They were not recent converts. To them the great verities of the faith should have been perfectly familiar; yet to them the very simplest of these realities had become dim and indistinct: "When by reason of the time ye ought to be teachers, ye have need again that some one teach you the rudiments of the first principles of the oracles of God." They needed to be taught the very ABC's of the gospel. Anything less elementary they were unable to understand. They were like infants whose sole article of diet must be milk, who are so undeveloped as to be unable to partake of any stronger nourishment. They were "such as have need of milk, and not of solid food." Their inability to be taught more advanced doctrines was the proof of their spiritual infancy: "For every one that partaketh of milk is without experience of the word of righteousness; for he is a babe." He cannot teach; he cannot even understand "the word of righteousness," that is, the divine message which results in the right conduct and in holy character; for spiritual infancy is marked not only by lack of knowledge but by imperfection of life.

On the other hand, "solid food is for fullgrown men, even those who by reason of use have their senses exercised to discern good and evil." That is to say, the more advanced doctrines are adapted to the more mature Christians, whose spiritual faculties have been so developed that they are able to discriminate between teaching that is wholesome and teaching that is harmful. Such Christians can appreciate and appropriate the more profound truths concerning Christ which the author is planning to disclose.

These references to spiritual infancy are not to be understood as disparaging the reality of a new birth or the blessedness of spiritual childhood. All persons begin the Christian life as mere "babes in Christ." There is a radiant beauty about each newborn soul. What the author does deprecate is arrested development. An infant is lovable, but if as the years pass the child remains a helpless babe, the case is pitiful and pathetic. Thus it is sad to see men and women, who for years have been professed Christians, to whom the deeper spiritual realities have no meaning, no power, no appeal.

Nor yet does the author mean to disparage the elementary truths of Christianity, "the rudiments of the first principles of the oracles of God," when he designates these as "milk" for "babes." There is a period of life when milk is the only possible diet, but it would be a sad experience if one never became able to receive nourishment of any other kind. So, too, there are truths perfectly adapted to those who are beginning the Christian life, but there are also more difficult doctrines, which support and develop the lives of more mature believers.

What the writer does intend to emphasize is the fact that use is a law of growth. The faculty which is never exercised grows weak. The talent which is unemployed is lost. Thus the simplest knowledge of Christ may be so appropriated, so appreciated, so comprehended, as to prepare one for the reception of more advanced teaching. On the other hand, the neglect or disregard of Christian truth may result in such a loss of discernment, such an atrophy of the faculties, as to induce a second childhood, a pitiable spiritual infancy. Of such infancy the author proposes two tests: the first is the inability to instruct others; the second is the inability to discern between the true and the false in religious teaching. By such tests the first readers of the epistle were rebuked. It is just possible that some of its modern readers may need the warning which the words contain.

(2) The Peril of Apostasy Ch. 6:1-8

1 Wherefore leaving the doctrine of the first principles of Christ, let us press on unto perfection; not laying again a foundation of repentance from dead works, and of faith toward God, 2 of the teaching of baptisms, and of laying on of hands, and of resurrection of the dead, and of eternal judgment. 3 And this will we do, if God permit. 4 For as touching those who were once enlightened and tasted of the heavenly gift, and were made partakers of the Holy Spirit, 5 and tasted the good word of God, and the powers of the age to come, 6 and then fell away, it is impossible to renew them again unto repentance; seeing they crucify to

*themselves the Son of God afresh, and put him to an open
shame. 7 For the land which hath drunk the rain that
cometh oft upon it, and bringeth forth herbs meet for them
for whose sake it is also tilled, receiveth blessing from God:
8 but if it beareth thorns and thistles, it is rejected and
nigh unto a curse; whose end is to be burned.*

Failure to advance in Christian knowledge results in an
infantile inability to apprehend truth. The faculty of hearing is dulled by disuse. Such failure is attended by an
even greater danger, namely, that of complete abandonment of the Christian faith, of an absolute apostasy from
Christ.

It is in view of this peril that the author urges his readers
to turn from the primary elements of Christian truth and
to advance toward a fuller knowledge. His specific desire
is that they may be aroused to receive his teaching concerning the high priesthood of Christ.

"Wherefore," since elementary teaching belongs to a
stage which long ago should have been passed, "leaving
the doctrine of the first principles of Christ, let us press on
unto perfection." The writer does not mean that these
simpler teachings are to be forgotten, or denied, or neglected, but that the attention is not to be limited to them.

The "perfection" to be sought consists, not in a state
of moral attainment, but in maturity of knowledge. It
denotes the condition of "fullgrown men" to whom the
writer has previously referred, men who can receive the
deeper truths concerning Christ, in contrast with "babes"
who must be fed with "milk."

Rather startling it is to note the list of doctrines which
the writer now adds as illustrating mere elementary teaching. These doctrines form the sole topics on which many
ministers dwell. In fact, some even pride themselves on
the fact that they are preaching the "simple gospel," when
confining themselves to only one or two of these doctrines.
They fail to realize that their choice of themes reveals
their own immaturity, and that their congregations are

receiving no "solid food," but only "milk."

The elementary Christian doctrines named by the writer are six in number, and are arranged in three series of two each. They concern conversion or the entrance upon the Christian life; ordinances, or church ceremonies; and prophecy, or the events of the last days.

In the first group are mentioned "repentance from dead works" and "faith toward God." These belong to the initial stage of Christian experience. "Repentance" is here characterized as "from dead works"; that is, not only from sins but even from good works done in mere obedience to law or to win merit, aside from any vital relation to God. Thus the remedy for such lifeless works is "faith toward God." This faith does not mean mere belief in the existence or the power of God, but trust in him and an acceptance of his grace revealed in Christ. Repentance and faith are absolutely essential; yet they form only a small segment of Christian doctrine. A man may be quite immature who is radiantly eager on all occasions to relate the experience of his conversion, and a preacher may be offering little "solid food" as he continually urges his hearers to turn from sin and to accept Christ.

"The teaching of baptisms, and . . . laying on of hands" is likewise important. Yet it is elementary. The rites and ceremonies of the church must be properly administered; yet one may manifest his Christian immaturity by his undue emphasis upon the form of baptism, or the formulas of confirmation, or the conditions and methods of ordination.

The "resurrection of the dead" and "eternal judgment" are necessary and essential truths. These and other themes related to the return of Christ and the end of the age are totally neglected by some teachers. On the other hand, there are those who dwell so exclusively upon these elements of prophecy as to neglect other truths and defraud their hearers of spiritual food far more needful for their nourishment and their growth as followers of Christ.

All these truths are fundamental. As the author declares, they form "a foundation." Yet he pleads with his readers to cease fixing their attention on those primary teachings in which in time past they have been well instructed, and to advance to higher stages of knowledge. "And this will we do," the writer adds hopefully, "if God permit," or with the blessing of God.

There is a dreadful alternative. If a person does not progress, he will relapse. If he fails to advance, he is in danger of going backward and of forsaking Christ altogether. Therefore the author solemnly warns his readers that if they have made a beginning in the Christian life and now turn from Christ and his gospel, they will find no other means of salvation. They never again can be brought to repentance.

Around this solemn warning ceaseless and needless controversy has been waged. Does it mean that one who has been saved can be lost? Or does it teach that one who has "fallen away from grace" can never repent? Taken out of their connection and pressed to their logical limits the words may be made to support either of these propositions. However, this would be to misinterpret the spirit and purpose of the author. He is not intending to raise obstruse questions in philosophy or in theology. This warning is to be taken in connection with the other similar warnings which express the main purpose of the epistle. It is a practical exhortation addressed to those who are in danger of neglecting, and so of losing, their knowledge of Christian truth. It is designed to keep the readers loyal to Christ and true to his gospel, as it points out the absolute hopelessness of apostasy.

The persons whose defection the author fears are described as "those who were once enlightened," that is, in a knowledge of the truth concerning Christ; "and tasted of the heavenly gift," the gift of eternal life which they had personally experienced; "and were made partakers of the Holy Spirit," sharing not only in the normal blessings of his indwelling presence but probably also endowed with those miraculous gifts which he bestowed upon the members of the early church; "and tasted the good word of God," having realized the goodness and beauty of the gospel message; "and the powers of the age to come," being so identified with Christ that they can be said to have shared the spiritual forces of the future age.

The description is undoubtedly that of persons who have entered upon the blessed experiences of a Christian life; yet of them the writer adds the words, "And then fell away." His words surely imply that such a fate might be conceived. However, it should be noted that he neither affirms nor denies that true Christians do thus fall away. He is presupposing an experience which he is sure will not be realized in the case of even the dull and indifferent readers whom he is addressing. (V. 9.) He is seeking to arouse them out of their lethargy. Therefore he adds, "It is impossible to renew them again unto repentance." To turn from Christ would be to take a step which is final and irrevocable. Repentance would be impossible because of the moral condition of the apostate: "Seeing they crucify to themselves the Son of God afresh, and put him to an open shame." Their turning away from Christ would place them on the side of those who rejected him and nailed him to a cross. It would be consenting to the judgment of his adversaries, to their blasphemies and cruelties in putting him to death. It would be "impossible to renew them again unto repentance"; there would be no new gospel to present, no new motives to which to appeal.

To show the hopeless condition and the just condemnation of those who thus thanklessly disregard Christ and his salvation, the author presents an analogy from nature. Land which receives abundant showers and is carefully tilled by man will bring forth abundant harvests; "but if it beareth thorns and thistles, it is rejected and nigh unto a curse; whose end is to be burned." Such is a law of human life. The use of divine gifts issues in greater blessings, but their neglect can result only in condemnation and in loss. No peril can compare with that of falling away from Christ and despising the gospel of his grace and love.

(3) Encouragement and Hope   Ch. 6:9-20

9 But, beloved, we are persuaded better things of you, and things that accompany salvation, though we thus speak: 10 for God is not unrighteous to forget your work and the love which ye showed toward his name, in that ye ministered unto the saints, and still do minister. 11 And we desire that each one of you may show the same diligence unto the fulness of hope even to the end: 12 that ye be not sluggish, but imitators of them who through faith and patience inherit the promises.

13 For when God made promise to Abraham, since he could swear by none greater, he sware by himself, 14 saying, Surely blessing I will bless thee, and multiplying I will mutliply thee. 15 And thus, having patiently endured, he obtained the promise. 16 For men swear by the greater: and in every dispute of theirs the oath is final for confirmation. 17 Wherein God, being minded to show more abundantly unto the heirs of the promise the immutability of his counsel, interposed with an oath; 18 that by two immutable things, in which it is impossible for God to lie, we may have a strong encouragement, who have fled for refuge to lay hold of the hope set before us: 19 which we have as an anchor of the soul, a hope both sure and stedfast and entering into that which is within the veil; 20 whither as a forerunner Jesus entered for us, having become a high priest for ever after the order of Melchizedek.

The rebuke has been severe. The warning has been solemn. Yet the situation is not desperate. The author has intimated that the indifference of his readers to Christian truth might result in their falling away from Christ. Yet this he cannot believe possible. He shrinks back from the very picture he has sketched. "But, beloved," he writes, "we are persuaded better things of you, and things that accompany salvation, though we thus speak." For his readers, as for all who have Christ as Savior, he entertains unfailing hope. He encourages them to cultivate a more confident assurance in their own hearts. His own expectation for them is based on the love which they previously have manifested. This love has been shown toward their fellow Christians, to whose needs they have ministered. Such love is a proof of spiritual life. God cannot fail to recognize and to strengthen that life which has been revealed in their service of his own people: "For God is not unrighteous to forget your work and the love which ye showed toward his name, in that ye ministered unto the saints, and still do minister."

The desire of the author is that his readers may enjoy a confidence in Christ which is more perfect and complete. He would have them to "abound in hope" as they have abounded in love, so that the dullness which has affected their understanding may not dwarf their spiritual growth. It is his earnest wish that their hope may be so fully developed that they may become imitators of those who through faith and long-suffering inherit that salvation which Christ now provides, and which will be complete when he again appears. Or, in the words of the author, "We desire that each one of you may show the same diligence unto the fulness of hope even to the end: that ye be not sluggish, but imitators of them who through faith and patience inherit the promises."

Their Christian hope will not deceive them. It is certain of fulfillment, for it is based on the sure word of God. An illustration of triumphant faith and a proof of the unfailing accomplishment of the divine promises are found in the case of Abraham. He is the Father of the Faithful, and ultimately, in the blessings bestowed upon believers, the promise made to him will be fully realized.

This promise was divinely confirmed. Those which Christians inherit, as heirs of Abraham, are equally sure. Abraham was told to expect that his descendants would be countless and that in him all the peoples of the earth would be blessed. This promise God confirmed by an oath taken in the name of his sacred honor: "For when God made promise to Abraham, since he could swear by none greater, he swore by himself, saying, Surely blessing I will bless thee, and multiplying I will multiply thee." On the part of Abraham patience and trust were required, but, "having patiently endured, he obtained the promise."

Just as men commonly take oaths, by which they confirm their statements in the name of some one greater than themselves, so God, in order to give absolute assurance to his people, confirmed his promise by an oath. Thus to us, who through Christ inherit the promise made to Abraham and his seed, God has given a double assurance—his promise and his oath—"that by two immutable things, in which it is impossible for God to lie, we may have a strong encouragement, who have fled for refuge to lay hold of the hope set before us." Our hope is of salvation in Christ, a hope of present security and deliverance, a hope of future glory. This hope "we have as an anchor of the soul, a hope both sure and stedfast and entering into that which is within the veil." An anchor is the accepted symbol of hope. As it enables a ship to outride the storms, so our Christian hope holds us secure through all the tempests of life; it can neither break nor drag. The anchor reaches down through the dark waters to grapple the unseen bed of the ocean; our hope rises into the sphere of the heavenly and eternal, into the Holy Place of the divine presence, to rest on God himself. Thither Jesus has ascended, and we shall follow him. "As a forerunner" he has "entered for us." He is the "Herald and Guarantee of our entrance." As our Advocate and Priest he has made atonement for sin, and now in his unceasing office, at the right hand of God, he secures access for us, "having become a high priest for ever after the order of Melchizedek."

c. The Melchizedek Priesthood   Ch. 7

(1) Melchizedek and Abraham   Ch. 7:1-10

1 For this Melchizedek, king of Salem, priest of God Most High, who met Abraham returning from the slaughter of the kings and blessed him, 2 to whom also Abraham divided a tenth part of all (being first, by interpretation, King of righteousness, and then also King of Salem, which is, King of peace; 3 without father, without mother, without genealogy, having neither beginning of days nor end of life, but made like unto the Son of God), abideth a priest continually.

4 Now consider how great this man was, unto whom Abraham, the patriarch, gave a tenth out of the chief spoils. 5 And they indeed of the sons of Levi that receive the priest's office have commandment to take tithes of the people according to the law, that is, of their brethren, though these have come out of the loins of Abraham: 6 but he whose genealogy is not counted from them hath taken tithes of Abraham, and hath blessed him that hath the promises. 7 But without any dispute the less is blessed of the better. 8 And here men that die receive tithes; but there one, of whom it is witnessed that he liveth. 9 And, so to say, through Abraham even Levi, who receiveth tithes, hath paid tithes; 10 for he was yet in the loins of his father, when Melchizedek met him.

The majestic figure of Melchizedek stands for one short scene upon the stage of history and then disappears forever into the mystery from which it emerged. However, an unfading halo of glory surrounds his very name, for this royal priest is an accepted type of Christ. His story is regarded as foreshadowing the essential feature in the priesthood of our Lord, namely, its abiding efficacy. Indeed, it is interpreted as attesting the finality of the Christian faith.

The story is short. Abraham had rescued Lot from Chedorlaomer and his confederates. Returning home, he was met on the way by "Melchizedek king of Salem . . .

priest of God Most High." By him Abraham was blessed, and to him he gave tithes of all the spoil. (Gen. 14:18-20.)

This fragment of history is interpreted as symbolizing the person and work of Christ. Melchizedek means "king of righteousness," and Salem, the name of his city, means "peace"; so that the very title points to him who is at once the King of Righteousness and the Prince of Peace. Christ, like Melchizedek, is a universal priest, whose priesthood is limited to no tribe or race, and he is at once both a Priest and a King. However, the point of comparison on which the writer dwells is the permanence of their priesthood. In the story of Melchizedek, no mention is made of his ancestry or his priestly pedigree, of his birth or his death. This silence is taken as an illustration of the eternal and changeless priesthood of Christ.

The writer does not mean that Melchizedek was immortal. Merely, as far as the story goes, he was "without father, without mother, without genealogy, having neither beginning of days nor end of life." In this respect, as presented in the narrative, he was "made like unto the Son of God," who, even more truly than Melchizedek, "abideth a priest continually" (Heb. 7:3).

Thus, by this story of Melchizedek, the discussion of the priesthood of Christ is resumed. It was begun by a statement of the qualifications of a high priest (ch. 5:1-10) and by a solemn warning against falling away from Christ (chs. 5:11 to 6:20). Both sections closed with the words of the psalmist to the effect that the priesthood of the Messiah was to be "after the order of Melchizedek." Therefore the writer now dwells upon the priesthood of Melchizedek to establish the point of this entire section (chs. 5 to 7), namely, the superiority of the priesthood of Christ to the priesthood of Aaron. The middle term of comparison is the priesthood of Melchizedek; and the reasoning is quite plain: The priesthood of Christ is "after the order of Melchizedek," but Melchizedek was superior to Aaron; therefore Christ is superior to Aaron.

This superiority of Melchizedek to Aaron is established by the fact that Abraham, the ancestor of Levi and of Aaron, who came from the tribe of Levi, paid tithes to Melchizedek and was blessed by Melchizedek. The receiving of tithes indicated a certain preeminence. Even in the case of the Levitical priests it implied a relative superiority to their brethren, who also were the descendants of Abraham and therefore equal in rank; but Melchizedek, whose priesthood did not depend upon human descent, received tithes from Abraham himself. Thus the Levitical priests, the descendants of Aaron, rendered homage to Melchizedek in the person of their ancestor, Abraham. Furthermore, the Levitical priests who received tithes from their brethren were subject to death; but no mention of Melchizedek's death is made in the Old Testament story.

So, too, Melchizedek's superiority is implied in the matter of the blessing he gave to Abraham. Aaron and the other Levitical priests shared in the blessings promised to Abraham; Melchizedek blessed Abraham, and "without any dispute the less is blessed of the better."

Thus, both in imparting a blessing and in receiving tithes, Melchizedek was seen to be superior to Abraham. Therefore, Christ, who was of the same order as Melchizedek, was superior to the Levitical, or Aaronic, priests, who were descended from Abraham.

Here, also, is an implied message for the followers of Christ: If his abiding and unchanging priesthood is typified by the priesthood of Melchizedek, then he may be expected to bless all those who, like Abraham, are true servants of God; and all who receive blessings from him should render him honor and homage, even as Abraham offered to Melchizedek tithes of the chief spoils of war.

(2) Christ and Aaron   Ch. 7:11-25

11 Now if there was perfection through the Levitical priesthood (for under it hath the people received the law), what further need was there that another priest should arise

*after the order of Melchizedek, and not be reckoned after
the order of Aaron?   12 For the priesthood being changed,
there is made of necessity a change also of the law.   13
For he of whom these things are said belongeth to another
tribe, from which no man hath given attendance at the
altar.   14 For it is evident that our Lord hath sprung out
of Judah; as to which tribe Moses spake nothing concerning priests.   15 And* what we say *is yet more abundantly
evident, if after the likeness of Melchizedek there ariseth
another priest, 16 who hath been made, not after the law
of a carnal commandment, but after the power of an endless life: 17 for it is witnessed* of him,*

  Thou art a priest for ever
  After the order of Melchizedek.*

*18 For there is a disannulling of a foregoing command-
ment because of its weakness and unprofitableness 19 (for
the law made nothing perfect), and a bringing in thereupon
of a better hope, through which we draw nigh unto God.
20 And inasmuch as* it is *not without the taking of an oath
21 (for they indeed have been made priests without an
oath; but he with an oath by him that saith of him,*

  The Lord sware and will not repent himself,
  Thou art a priest for ever);*

*22 by so much also hath Jesus become the surety of a bet-
ter covenant.   23 And they indeed have been made priests
many in number, because that by death they are hindered
from continuing: 24 but he, because he abideth for ever,
hath his priesthood unchangeable.   25 Wherefore also he
is able to save to the uttermost them that draw near unto
God through him, seeing he ever liveth to make intercession for them.*

It has already been indicated that the priesthood of
Christ is superior to that of Aaron and of all the Levitical
priests.   The writer now proves that the priesthood of
Christ supersedes the priesthood of Aaron.   This is implied
in the very prediction that Christ was to be "a high priest
after the order of Melchizedek."   If the Aaronic priesthood had accomplished all it promised or prefigured, there
would have been no necessity for the coming of a Priest

belonging to a different order. His coming implies that the former priesthood is done away with and is no longer in effect. Yet this Levitical or Aaronic priesthood was the essential feature in the Mosaic law. Therefore in the person and work of Christ that entire system was brought to an end.

"Now if there was perfection through the Levitical priesthood (for under it hath the people received the law)," the writer contends, "what further need was there that another priest should arise after the order of Melchizedek?" "Perfection" here denotes a right relation to God, or the reconciliation of men to God. This involves the removal of sin, which lies as an obstacle preventing free access to God and fellowship with him. Such reconciliation the Levitical priesthood could typify and predict but could not secure. Therefore, of necessity, it must give way to another priesthood. This doctrine was clearly understood by the author of the psalm, who enjoyed all the privileges the Levitical priesthood could provide. He predicted the coming of a Priest "after the order of Melchizedek." Yet the priesthood constituted the very soul of the Mosaic system. Therefore, as our writer insists, "the priesthood being changed, there is made of necessity a change also of the law." (Vs. 11-12.)

That so great a change had been made, that a Priest had arisen who could reconcile men to God, that Moses had been superseded by Christ, was evidenced by the fact that the Priest who had come "after the order of Melchizedek" belonged to the tribe of Judah and not to the tribe of Levi. "For he of whom these things are said belongeth to another tribe, from which no man hath given attendance at the altar. For it is evident that our Lord hath sprung out of Judah; as to which tribe Moses spake nothing concerning priests." (Vs. 13-14.)

That with this change in the priesthood the whole Mosaic economy has disappeared is still further proved by the nature of the new Priest, and the unique basis on which his office rests. He was not made a priest by a rule or statute but in virtue of an inherent, imperishable life, so that his priesthood is described as changeless and imperishable. Or, to use the words of the writer, "What we say is yet more abundantly evident, if after the likeness of Melchizedek there ariseth another priest, who hath been made, not after the law of a carnal commandment, but after the power of an endless life: for it is witnessed of him,

> "Thou art a priest for ever
> After the order of Melchizedek."

This difference between the priesthood of Aaron and the Melchizedek priesthood of Christ is thus strikingly drawn. The former rested on a regulation that men should be appointed priests because they were sons of certain parents. Their appointment, therefore, did not depend upon their spiritual fitness or their personal desire. They served in obedience to a law of mere physical descent, "the law of a carnal commandment." Very different was the priesthood of Christ. He served, not because of any external compulsion, but because impelled and enabled by an inner power, the power of a life which death could not dissolve.

That Christ does possess such inherent energy, that his priesthood is eternal, that Christianity is not to be superseded, is proved by a quotation from The Psalms:

> "Thou art a priest for ever
> After the order of Melchizedek."

Already (vs. 1-3) the writer has shown that Melchizedek typified the changeless priesthood of Christ. Now, however, he quotes the term "for ever." "The order of Melchizedek" would imply continuance and permanence; but the idea is emphasized and confirmed by the words of the psalmist, "Thou art a priest for ever."

However, before dwelling upon the perpetuity of Christ's priesthood (vs. 23-25) the writer reverts to the contrast between the "carnal commandment" on which the Aaronic priesthood rested and "the power of an endless life" which characterized the priesthood of Christ (v. 16).

The results of superseding the one by the other were twofold. First, "there is a disannulling of a foregoing commandment because of its weakness and unprofitableness." The old, imperfect priesthood, which was based on a mere external law of fleshly descent, passes away. It does so because of its uselessness and helplessness in the matter of bringing sinful man into spiritual fellowship with a holy God. With it, too, passes the whole legal system of which it was the characteristic feature, "for the law made nothing perfect." The law did have its place and function. It was preparatory, instructive, prophetic. Yet it brought nothing to perfection. It failed to bring man into right relation with God.

Then, secondly, there is "a bringing in thereupon of a better hope." This "better hope" is that of attaining the goal to which the law had pointed, the hope "through which we draw nigh unto God." It is better because it is effective.

It secures what the law had failed to provide, namely, a direct entrance into perfect fellowship with God. This hope springs from faith in Christ. Its very essence is in his priesthood and his person. It is the hope described by the writer in the previous chapter. It is "the hope set before us: which we have as an anchor of the soul, a hope both sure and stedfast and entering into that which is within the veil; whither as a forerunner Jesus entered for us, having become a high priest for ever after the order of Melchizedek" (ch. 6:18-20).

The superiority of this Melchizedek priesthood of Christ to the priesthood of Aaron is proved by still another fact. It was ratified by a solemn divine oath, which was absent from the ritual of the Levitical priesthood. This oath declared the priesthood of Christ to be permanent and changeless. "They indeed have been made priests without an oath; but he with an oath by him that saith of him,

"The Lord sware and will not repent himself,
Thou art a priest for ever."

The priesthood of Christ being final and eternal, and thus superior to the priesthood of Aaron, it follows that the covenant under which he ministers is far superior to the Old Testament system. "By so much also," the writer declares, "hath Jesus become the surety of a better covenant." This new covenant is not temporary and provisional, but abiding and effective and certain to secure the ends for which it was established, namely, the forgiveness of sins and the bringing of men into fellowship with God.

The writer dwells upon one further feature of superiority in the priesthood of Christ. It consists in the facts of the continuing life of the Priest, to which reference has already been made, and of the consequent ability of the Priest to save those who put their trust in him.

By way of contrast, the Levitical priests were ever changing, being compelled by death to give place to others in a ceaseless succession; whereas Christ, "because he abideth for ever, hath his priesthood unchangeable."

Such a qualification enables him "to save to the uttermost them that draw near unto God through him"; and this is true because his ministrations on their behalf never cease: "He ever liveth to make intercession for them." Thus the abiding and heavenly priesthood of Christ secures for the believers not only free and continual access to God but also a salvation which is complete. This is an "eternal salvation"; and "to the uttermost" denotes not merely duration but also quality. The salvation extends to the last element of man's being; it supplies every aspect of man's need. It secures present deliverance; it is perfected in future glory.

(3) The Ideal High Priest   Ch. 7:26-28

26 For such a high priest became us, holy, guileless, undefiled, separated from sinners, and made higher than the heavens; 27 who needeth not daily, like those high priests, to offer up sacrifices, first for his own sins, and then for the sins of the people: for this he did once for all, when he offered up himself. 28 For the law appointeth men high priests, having infirmity; but the word of the oath, which was after the law, appointeth a Son, perfected for evermore.

Now the writer gives a summary of all that he has said as to the priesthood of Christ, "after the order of Melchizedek," and contrasts this with the Levitical priesthood. Yet the paragraph is more than a summary. It forms a transition from the comparison of Christ with Melchizedek to the contrast between the atoning work of Christ and the ministry of the Aaronic high priest.

The statement has just been made that Christ "is able to save to the uttermost." The writer now adds that for this completion of our salvation we need, in the heavenly sanctuary, such a perfect High Priest as Christ. Since we are sinful and frail and dependent, we must have a Savior, a Mediator, a High Priest, in whom we can have perfect confidence, one who is "holy, guileless, undefiled, separated from sinners, and made higher than the heavens."

"Holy" describes his qualities of piety, or saintly obedience, of loyalty and humility and faith, to which reference has been made in earlier portions of the epistle. "Guileless" denotes not only innocence, but also the absence of any trait of malice or evil thought which might prompt him to disregard the needs of men. "Undefiled," or morally stainless, is in probable comparison with the scrupulous ritual purity of the Levitical high priest. These human perfections Christ retains even in his present exaltation. He is now "separated from sinners," free from any possible contamination, "and made higher than the heavens," in a sphere of celestial purity and glory, and in a position of universal power.

His ministry, like his moral character, is in striking contrast with that of the Levitical priesthood. The Levitical priests repeated their sacrifices again and again. The priests offered them daily, the high priest, to speak more exactly, year after year. Christ's sacrifice was made "once for all, when he offered up himself." Nor did he need, like them, to offer sacrifices for his own sins. He was sinless, "holy, guileless, undefiled." They were frail and sinful men, "for the law appointeth men high priests, having infirmity," but the Priest of the new covenant, whom God has appointed by his oath, is a Son, who by his human experiences and his heavenly exaltation has been fitted forever for his saving work, "perfected for evermore." Since "such a high priest" has been given us, we should turn from all other mediators, we should cease from all self-confidence, we should depend on no human rites or ceremonies, and should "draw near unto God through him," with unchanging devotion, with unfailing trust.

B. THE ATONING WORK   Chs. 8:1 to 10:18

1. THE HEAVENLY SANCTUARY   Ch. 8:1-6

1 Now in the things which we are saying the chief point is this: We have such a high priest, who sat down on the right hand of the throne of the Majesty in the heavens, 2 a minister of the sanctuary, and of the true tabernacle, which the Lord pitched, not man. 3 For every high priest is appointed to offer both gifts and sacrifices: wherefore it is necessary that this high priest also have somewhat to offer. 4 Now if he were on earth, he would not be a priest at all, seeing there are those who offer the gifts according to the law; 5 who serve that which is a copy and shadow of the heavenly things, even as Moses is warned of God when he is about to make the tabernacle: for, See, saith he, that thou make all things according to the pattern that was showed thee in the mount. 6 But now hath he obtained a ministry the more excellent, by so much as he is also the mediator of a better covenant, which hath been enacted upon better promises.

The eighth chapter marks a new division in the epistle. Previously the author has been describing the person and qualifications of the great High Priest; he now dwells upon his atoning work. That the purpose of the author was to present the salvation wrought by Christ under figures taken from the Jewish priesthood was stated in his introductory paragraph. (Ch. 1:3.) It was again indicated when he was comparing the mediation of Christ with that of the angels. (Ch. 2:17.)

It was further emphasized when Christ was shown to be superior to Moses and the other leaders of Israel. (Ch. 4:14-16.) With this thought of priesthood, the next chapters were wholly concerned. (Chs. 5 to 7.) Like Aaron and the Levitical priests, Christ was shown to be qualified for priestly service by human sympathy and divine appointment. (Ch. 5:1-10.) The readers were warned that an understanding of his person and work would demand patience and effort. (Chs. 5:11 to 6:20.) It was then shown that the priesthood of Christ was superior to that of Aaron, because it was after a higher order, namely, "the order of Melchizedek." (Ch. 7.)

Now, turning to the actual work of Christ, the author describes it as so superior to that of the Jewish priests as to indicate that by it the whole Mosaic economy is done away; in its place abides the absolute, eternal, perfect priesthood of Christ. It is noted first that the scene of Christ's ministry is the true sanctuary, a sanctuary not of earth but of heaven (ch. 8:1-6), and that it is performed under a new covenant, a covenant not of works but of grace (ch. 8:7-13).

Then the death and ascension and intercession of Christ are compared with the ritual of the Day of Atonement as observed by the Levitical priests. (Ch. 9.) Finally the thought is centered upon the sacrifice of Christ, the abiding efficacy of which is contrasted with the typical and repeated offerings of the Levitical priests. (Ch. 10:1-18.)

To begin with, the superior greatness of Christ's priesthood is indicated by the scene in which it is being exercised: "Now in the things which we are saying the chief point is this: We have such a high priest, who sat down on the right hand of the throne of the Majesty in the heavens, a minister of the sanctuary, and of the true tabernacle, which the Lord pitched, not man."

Thus Christ is at once a Priest and a King. He now occupies the place of supreme power. He is as much greater than the Levitical priests as the universe is greater than the contracted tent in which those priests were appointed to serve. He must be serving in such a heavenly, upper sanctuary; for he is a Priest, and as such must "have somewhat to offer"; and it cannot be on earth that he fulfills his priestly work, because the priestly office on earth is already filled. As the writer declares, "If he were on earth, he would not be a priest at all, seeing there are those who offer the gifts according to the law." His ministry is in the true sanctuary of which the tabernacle which Moses erected was but "a copy and shadow." That the latter was merely a type and symbol of realities, God plainly declared when directing Moses as to its erection: "See, saith he, that thou make all things according to the pattern that was showed thee in the mount."

It is needless to suppose that this pattern was visible, material, tangible. It is rather absurd to imagine that Moses when on Mt. Sinai was shown models of the tabernacle, ark, candlestick, or altar. Quite the opposite is the contention of the author of the epistle. He meant that these visible objects were but the types and shadows of invisible realities which were made plain to Moses. These realities included the holiness of God, access to God, the worship of God, the divine provision for moral cleansing, the necessity for mediation, for sacrifice, for intercession. These and similar great spiritual verities were impressed upon the mind of Moses and he was guided to erect a structure and to ordain a ritual by which these truths were set forth in symbol and in type. With these spiritual realities the priesthood of Christ is concerned. He so far surpasses the Levitical priests as substance surpasses shadow, as fulfillment surpasses prophecy, as a reality surpasses a type. The tabernacle in the wilderness was full of significance; yet all that it typified of the relation between men and God is fulfilled in the spiritual experiences made possible by the atoning work and continuing ministry of Jesus Christ.

However, Christ is not "on earth" (v. 4) but is exercising a heavenly priesthood which is as much superior to its earthly counterpart as the new dispensation with which it is connected is superior to the old, in the hopes and blessings which it offers. As the author declares, "But now hath he obtained a ministry the more excellent, by so much as he is also the mediator of a better covenant, which hath been enacted upon better promises."

The exact nature and excellencies of this "better covenant" are set forth by the author in the passage which follows (vs. 7-13). Suffice it here to say that the better covenant denotes the whole Christian system, as it fulfills and supersedes the system of Moses. Of this better covenant Christ is the Mediator. He combines the offices of Moses, who mediated the law, and of Aaron, the high priest who interceded with God for the people. All the blessings of the better covenant, all the promises and hopes, all its present benefits and future glories, are secured for believers by the mediating and heavenly ministry of Christ.

2. THE NEW COVENANT   Ch. 8:7-13

7 *For if that first* covenant *had been faultless, then would no place have been sought for a second.   8 For finding fault with them, he saith,*
  Behold, the days come, saith the Lord,
  That I will make a new covenant with the house of Israel and with the house of Judah;
9 *Not according to the covenant that I made with their fathers*
  In the day that I took them by the hand to lead them forth out of the land of Egypt;

> *For they continued not in my covenant,*
> *And I regarded them not, saith the Lord.*
> 10 *For this is the covenant that I will make with the house*
>   *of Israel*
>   *After those days, saith the Lord;*
>   *I will put my laws into their mind,*
>   *And on their heart also will I write them:*
>   *And I will be to them a God,*
>   *And they shall be to me a people:*
> 11 *And they shall not teach every man his fellow-citizen,*
>   *And every man his brother, saying, Know the Lord:*
>   *For all shall know me,*
>   *From the least to the greatest of them.*
> 12 *For I will be merciful to their iniquities,*
>   *And their sins will I remember no more.*
> 13 *In that he saith, A new* covenant, *he hath made the first*
> *old. But that which is becoming old and waxeth aged is*
> *nigh unto vanishing away.*

The superiority of the ministry of Christ to that of the Levitical priests is evident from the fact that it is exercised in a heavenly sanctuary, but also because it is related to a new and better covenant. The word "covenant" commonly denoted an agreement between two parties. Yet in a divine covenant the parties stand in no sense as equal contractors. God, in his grace, makes an arrangement which man receives. This was true of the old covenant as well as of the new; in either case there was a gracious disposition or arrangement. It was an expression of the will of God which was to be accepted by those to whom it was given. Unfortunately, the word was translated, in English versions, by the word "testament," which means a will, or an instrument that disposes of property according to the purpose of a testator. The Mosaic covenant forms so essential a feature of the Jewish Scriptures that these writings are called the "Old Testament." The covenant mediated by Christ is so central in the Christian Scriptures that the latter are called the "New Testament." The American Standard Version is more exact in printing on the title-page these words: "The New Covenant Commonly Called The New Testament." It is vain to hope that the correction will be adopted in describing the books of the Bible. However, it is helpful to be reminded that the old covenant and the new covenant are phrases which properly may be regarded as embodying the essential difference between Judaism and Christianity, between the old dispensation and the new, between Moses and Christ.

Both covenants were expressions of the divine will. Both were designed to bring men into fellowship with God. Why, then, was the old displaced by the new? The author of the epistle makes answer: (a) The first covenant failed to accomplish its purpose, because of the frailty of man. (b) Even the prophets of God who lived under the old predicted the establishment of a new covenant. (c) The very title "new" antiquated the "old."

The writer insists that if the Mosaic system had been perfect, it would not have been supplanted by a new dispensation: "For if that first covenant had been faultless, then would no place have been sought for a second." It did not bring men into abiding spiritual fellowship with God. Yet the cause of the failure lay in the character of the people, not in the law, which was holy, righteous, and good. It was imperfect only because it did not provide sufficiently against the imperfections which were in them. God did not find fault with the covenant; but "finding fault with them" he predicted the making of a new covenant.

An extended prediction of this kind is quoted from the prophecies of Jeremiah (Jer. 31:31-34). Here is foretold the making of a covenant which would be different from that which God had given on Mt. Sinai. The latter had failed through no lack of power and grace on the part of God, which was evident from the fact that he had just delivered the people from Egypt. This covenant had been abandoned by both parties:

> "For they continued not in my covenant,
> And I regarded them not, saith the Lord."

The marks of the new order which God was to establish would consist of three particulars: (1) It was to be a system of inner rather than of outer law, spiritual rather than external and formal:

> "I will put my laws into their mind,
> And on their heart also will I write them."

Instead of being graven on stone, the law of God would be written on the spirit and desires of men, so that their wills would be in harmony with the divine will:

> "And I will be to them a God,
> And they shall be to me a people."

(2) As a result there will be a universal and immediate knowledge of God. There will be no privileged class, or order, standing between God and men:

> "And they shall not teach every man his fellow-citizen,
> And every man his brother, saying, Know the Lord:
> For all shall know me,
> From the least to the greatest of them."

(3) The third characteristic of the new covenant is that it shall be a dispensation of grace and forgiveness. This is the supreme pledge of its efficacy:

> "For I will be merciful to their iniquities,
> And their sins will I remember no more."

Just how this pardon is to be provided, and who is to be the divine Sacrifice for sin, the next chapters will reveal. The present argument as to the new covenant closes here with the statement that it is soon to supersede the old. Speaking of a new covenant brands the former covenant as old. It implies that the old is inadequate. If the prophet so long ago could speak of the change from the old to the new as imminent, it must now be near its consummation; for "that which is becoming old and waxeth aged is nigh unto vanishing away."

3. THE WAY INTO THE HOLIEST   Ch. 9:1-10

1 Now even the first covenant *had ordinances of divine service, and its sanctuary,* a sanctuary *of this world. 2 For there was a tabernacle prepared, the first, wherein* were *the candlestick, and the table, and the showbread; which is called the Holy place. 3 And after the second veil, the tabernacle which is called the Holy of holies; 4 having a golden altar of incense, and the ark of the covenant overlaid round about with gold, wherein* was *a golden pot holding the manna, and Aaron's rod that budded, and the tables of the covenant; 5 and above it cherubim of glory overshadowing the mercy-seat; of which things we cannot now speak severally. 6 Now these things having been thus prepared, the priests go in continually into the first tabernacle, accomplishing the services; 7 but into the second the high priest alone, once in the year, not without blood, which he offereth for himself, and for the errors of the people: 8 the Holy Spirit this signifying, that the way into the holy place hath not yet been made manifest, while the first tabernacle is yet standing; 9 which* is *a figure for the time present; according to which are offered both gifts and sacrifices that cannot, as touching the conscience, make the worshipper perfect, 10* being *only (with meats and drinks and divers washings) carnal ordinances, imposed until a time of reformation.*

The writer is showing the superiority of the atoning work of Christ to the ministry of the Levitical priests. The scene in which Christ ministers is not that of an earthly sanctuary; it is the sphere of heavenly realities. The new covenant, in connection with which he serves, is one of grace and not of works. Turning now to the service itself, the ministry of Christ far surpasses that of the Levitical system even in the most impressive form of the latter as seen in the ritual of the great Day of Atonement. This very ritual pictured its own inefficiency. Especially was this true in its exclusion from the Holy of Holies of all but the high priest, who himself could enter only once a year. This was an indication that under the old economy the real purpose of religion, namely, the free access of man to God, was not attained.

In making this comparison the writer, with evident appreciation, dwells upon the dignity and glory of the ancient ordinances of worship. He describes in detail the tabernacle in the wilderness, the visible earthly sanctuary erected according to divine appointment. This tabernacle was of two parts, or consisted of two rooms, the outer one known as the Holy Place and, beyond a separating veil, the inner one, known as the Holy of Holies. In the former were the golden candlestick, the table of shewbread, and the altar of incense. In the latter was the Ark of the Covenant with its mercy seat and "cherubim of glory"; it was the place where the divine presence was manifested.

The author mentions the "golden altar of incense" as belonging to the Holy of Holies because of its close association with this most holy place in the ancient ritual. The altar represented worship; the Holy of Holies symbolized the manifestation of God. Thus the two are placed in immediate connection.

Having reminded his readers of the construction of the tabernacle, the writer now refers to the significant lesson which the prescribed use of its two rooms embodied. The priests were allowed to "go in continually into the first" of its rooms, but into the Holy of Holies "the high priest alone, once in the year," when he made atonement for his own sins and for those of the people. This arrangement, by which the most holy place was made so inaccessible, the Holy Spirit, the author of the ritual, employed as a symbolic expression of the fact that free access into the immediate presence of God was not yet possible, and therefore fellowship with God was not yet perfect. The outer room of the ancient tabernacle was therefore "a figure," or a parable, of the entire Mosaic dispensation in its failure to effect a full and free spiritual approach to God. Thus all the sacrifices offered under the old covenant failed in the full accomplishment of their purpose. They could not, "as

touching the conscience, make the worshipper perfect."
They were not able to give an inner sense of cleansing and
spiritual renewal and peace of heart. They were merely
outward and temporary. They had to do "with meats
. . . and divers washings." They were merely "ordinances" of the flesh and not of the spirit. They were imposed "until a time of reformation," a time when matters
would be brought into a satisfactory and permanent state,
the time of the new covenant. Only through Christ do
men find perfect fellowship with God, peace of conscience,
rest for their souls.

4. THE NECESSARY SACRIFICE   Ch. 9:11-22

*11 But Christ having come a high priest of the good
things to come, through the greater and more perfect tabernacle, not made with hands, that is to say, not of this creation, 12 nor yet through the blood of goats and calves, but
through his own blood, entered in once for all into the holy
place, having obtained eternal redemption. 13 For if the
blood of goats and bulls, and the ashes of a heifer sprinkling them that have been defiled, sanctify unto the cleanness of the flesh: 14 how much more shall the blood of
Christ, who through the eternal Spirit offered himself without blemish unto God, cleanse your conscience from dead
works to serve the living God? 15 And for this cause he
is the mediator of a new covenant, that a death having
taken place for the redemption of the transgressions that
were under the first covenant, they that have been called
may receive the promise of the eternal inheritance. 16 For
where a testament is, there must of necessity be the death
of him that made it. 17 For a testament is of force where
there hath been death: for it doth never avail while he that
made it liveth. 18 Wherefore even the first covenant hath
not been dedicated without blood. 19 For when every
commandment had been spoken by Moses unto all the
people according to the law, he took the blood of the calves
and goats, with water and scarlet wool and hyssop, and
sprinkled both the book itself and all the people, 20 saying, This is the blood of the covenant which God com-*

manded to you-ward. 21 Moreover the tabernacle and all
the vessels of the ministry he sprinkled in like manner with
the blood. 22 And according to the law, I may almost
say, all things are cleansed with blood, and apart from
shedding of blood there is no remission.

The Mosaic ordinances of worship bore on their surface
the marks of imperfection. They indicated their inadequacy to bring men into true fellowship with God. However, they were prophetic of a better economy under which
this fellowship would be complete. This ideal system,
toward which the ancient ordinances pointed, has been introduced by Christ. His ministry has been performed in
the sphere of divine realities, in "the greater and more perfect tabernacle," not in one "made with hands" or "of this
creation," not in one which was merely symbolic, temporary, earthly.

So, too, the sacrifice he offered was not that of "the
blood of goats and calves," but that of his own life. By
virtue of his atoning blood he "entered in once for all into
the holy place," into the very presence of God, "having
obtained eternal redemption." It was thus, by offering
himself, that Christ secured for us salvation, deliverance
from the guilt and pollution of sin, and unending fellowship with God. This salvation is "eternal," in contrast
with the effect of the repeated offerings of the ancient
ritual.

The contrast between the old and the new, between the
atonement of the law and the atonement of Christ, is
heightened and expanded in the remaining paragraphs of
this chapter. The writer dwells first upon the purifying
power of Christ's sacrifice. This is effective because accomplished in the sphere, not of external ordinances, but
of spiritual realities. Such is the argument of the next two
verses: "For if the blood of goats and bulls, and the ashes
of a heifer sprinkling them that have been defiled, sanctify
unto the cleanness of the flesh: how much more shall the
blood of Christ, who through the eternal Spirit offered him-

self without blemish unto God, cleanse your conscience from dead works to serve the living God?" That is, if the sacrifice of animals accomplished a ceremonial cleansing, how much more shall the spiritual sacrifice of Christ purify the soul!

The author here still refers to the ritual of the Day of Atonement, with its offerings of "goats and bulls," described in Lev., ch. 16, and also to an ordinance, recorded in Num., ch. 19, according to which a person who had been defiled by contact with the dead, and so debarred from the privilege of worship, might be cleansed and so restored to fellowship with the people of God. This was effected by the "water for impurity," in which had been placed the ashes of a sacrifice. When sprinkled with this water the unclean was again sanctified.

With such an outward, ritual purification the writer contrasts the cleansing power of "the blood of Christ." His sacrifice was voluntary, it was rational, it was by action of "the eternal Spirit." For this reason it was effectual in the sphere of the spiritual and the eternal. It could secure "eternal redemption." It could "cleanse [the] conscience from dead works," from works which defile the soul, as contact with a dead body made the ancient worshiper unclean. The purpose or result of such spiritual cleansing as Christ effects is that the one so purified may "serve the living God," may enter into fellowship with him, and render him the priestly service of a holy life. (Heb. 9:13-14.)

"For this cause," that is, since his perfect sacrifice cleanses the "conscience" and brings men to God, "he is the mediator of a new covenant." Under the old covenant atonement for sins had been typical and symbolic; yet the true atonement of Christ, which is the foundation of the new covenant, avails for those who lived under the old imperfect Jewish dispensation. His death secures "the redemption of the transgressions that were under the first covenant." The people of God in Old Testament days had been promised an "inheritance." A gospel had been preached to them. (Ch. 4:2.)   This "eternal inheritance," this perfect salvation, could not be enjoyed until the sacrifice of Christ, which establishes the new covenant, had been made. (Ch. 9:15.)

This sacrifice was absolutely necessary: "For where a testament is, there must of necessity be the death of him that made it."   Here the writer seems to play upon the word which may be translated either "covenant" or "testament."   Many interpreters prefer to retain the translation "covenant," which is the uniform use in Scripture.   It is true, indeed, that covenants were usually confirmed by sacrifices which involved the expense of life.   In this sense the death of Christ was necessary to the establishment of the new covenant.   However, it is obvious that the one who makes a covenant does not actually die.   Christ did actually offer himself as the true Sacrifice.   The absolute necessity of his death could not be expressed by saying that a covenant must be sealed by a vicarious offering.   His death was as necessary to the establishment of the new covenant as the death of a testator is to the putting in force of a "last will and testament."   "For a testament is of force where there hath been death: for it doth never avail while he that made it liveth."   (V. 17.)

However, both the old covenant and the new were of the nature of gracious, divine arrangements or dispositions.   In both cases death was necessary.   In establishing the new covenant it was the death of Christ.   In the case of the old it was the offering of animal sacrifices.   In this particular the requirement was the same.   "Wherefore even the first covenant," the writer declares, "hath not been dedicated without blood."   At the time of its solemn ratification, "when every commandment had been spoken by Moses unto all the people according to the law, he took the blood of the calves and the goats, with water and scarlet wool and hyssop, and sprinkled both the book itself and all the people, saying, This is the blood of the covenant which God commanded to you-ward.   Moreover the tabernacle and all the vessels of the ministry he sprinkled in like manner with the blood. And according to the law, I may almost say, all things are cleansed with blood, and apart from shedding of blood there is no remission."

Such a statement of the principle of expiation by the shedding of blood in connection with the first covenant is used by the writer to illustrate the absolute necessity of the sacrificial death of Christ in order to establish the new covenant under which remission of sins and access to God were made possible.

There is a deep significance in the words of Moses, which the author quotes: "This is the blood of the covenant." They recall the words used by our Lord in instituting the Supper which ever after was to be a memorial of his atoning death: "And he took a cup, and gave thanks, and gave to them, saying, Drink ye all of it; for this is my blood of the covenant, which is poured out for many unto remission of sins."

5. THE MEDIATION AND REAPPEARING OF CHRIST
Ch. 9:23-28

23 It was necessary therefore that the copies of the things in the heavens should be cleansed with these; but the heavenly things themselves with better sacrifices than these. 24 For Christ entered not into a holy place made with hands, like in pattern to the true; but into heaven itself, now to appear before the face of God for us: 25 nor yet that he should offer himself often, as the high priest entereth into the holy place year by year with blood not his own; 26 else must he often have suffered since the foundation of the world: but now once at the end of the ages hath he been manifested to put away sin by the sacrifice of himself. 27 And inasmuch as it is appointed unto men once to die, and after this cometh *judgment; 28 so Christ also, having been once offered to bear the sins of many, shall appear a second time, apart from sin, to them that wait for him, unto salvation.*

There were two essential features in the ritual of the great Day of Atonement. (Lev., ch. 16.) The first was the offering of sacrifices. The second was the entrance of the high priest into the Holy of Holies to appear for the people in the presence of God. Both these features of the ancient ritual found their fulfillment in the atoning work of Christ. Upon the first the writer has been dwelling. He has been showing the absolute necessity of Christ's death. To that fact he now reverts. Then attention will be directed to the entrance of the great High Priest into the heavenly sanctuary, and to his subsequent return.

That the ancient tabernacle, and all its symbols of approach to God, needed to be sanctified by sacrifice and by the sprinkling of blood has been seen to be a necessary requirement of the Mosaic law. It is argued, by analogy, that the holy place on high must be made accessible for believers by a more perfect sacrifice, namely, by the death of Christ himself: "It was necessary therefore that the copies of the things in the heavens should be cleansed with these; but the heavenly things themselves with better sacrifices than these." The offering of animals might avail in a system of types and shadows; but in the sphere of spiritual and eternal realities there must be a nobler form of cleansing, and a spiritual sacrifice in virtue of which men may be brought into immediate fellowship with God. (V. 23.)

"For Christ entered not into a holy place made with hands," one which like that of the Jewish tabernacle was a mere "pattern" of "the true," a symbol of the divine presence. He has entered "into heaven itself, now to appear before the face of God for us." By way of death he has passed into a state of immediate, celestial fellowship with God. He enjoys a vision which is direct and absolute. Yet this is not for his own enjoyment. It is that he may provide "for us" (v. 24) pardon, and peace, and abiding communion with God.

Unlike the service of the Jewish high priest, the atoning work of Christ need not be repeated. It is of absolute value. It avails for all sin, past and present and future. Had his sacrifice been like that of the old covenant, it would have had to be offered again and again to meet the needs of men.

"Nor yet that he should offer himself often," the writer explains, "as the high priest entereth into the holy place year by year with blood not his own; else must he often have suffered since the foundation of the world: but now once at the end of the ages hath he been manifested to put away sin by the sacrifice of himself." The time of this manifestation is declared to be "at the end of the ages," indicating the climax and consummation of long periods of preparation, of symbolism, of prophecy, of expectation. The purpose of this manifestation was "to put away sin," to abolish it, to put it aside, to destroy it with all its effects. It was thus to remove every barrier and to bring men into the heavenly fellowship with God which the ancient ritual foreshadowed. This was accomplished by the death of Christ, "by the sacrifice of himself." (Vs. 25-26.)

To emphasize his statement that this death of Christ is not to be repeated but is "once for all," the author appeals to the fact that men die once for all. Death is not repeated, nor is it followed by a return to earth, but subsequently by judgment. Yet here there is a startling contrast. The death of Christ is not to be repeated, but he is to return to earth. He is to appear a second time, literally to be made "visible to the eye." The writer states, "And inasmuch as it is appointed unto men once to die, and after this cometh judgment; so Christ also, having been once offered to bear the sins of many, shall appear a second time, apart from sin, to them that wait for him, unto salvation." This future appearing is to be "apart from sin," not again to deal with sin, not to be an offering for sin, but to complete the salvation of his followers, who here are described as "them that wait for him." On the Day of Atonement the high priest laid aside his garments of glory and beauty, and clothed only in white linen performed his sacrificial task and entered into the Holy of Holies; but when he reappeared to the expectant people he was again clothed in his resplendent robes. So Christ laid aside his garments of heavenly splendor and appeared on earth in the garb of spotless manhood to accomplish his atoning work. Then he entered the heavenly sanctuary, opening for man a way of spiritual access to God. Yet some day, to his expectant followers, he is to reappear in robes of imperial majesty, not to suffer for sins but to bring to a consummation the salvation promised to those who put their trust in him.

Thus this paragraph (vs. 23-28) relates three appearings or manifestations of Christ. Together they summarize his atoning work. First, he was "manifested to put away sin by the sacrifice of himself," when he came into the world to suffer and to die as the Redeemer of mankind. Then, he "entered . . . into heaven itself, now to appear before the face of God for us" as our Mediator and Intercessor, making access and fellowship possible and complete. Then again, he "shall appear a second time," in power and great glory, the returning Savior, the reigning, rewarding, triumphant King.

6. THE FINAL SACRIFICE   Ch. 10:1-18

1 For the law having a shadow of the good things to come, not the very image of the things, can never with the same sacrifices year by year, which they offer continually, make perfect them that draw nigh. 2 Else would they not have ceased to be offered? because the worshippers, having been once cleansed, would have had no more consciousness of sins. 3 But in those sacrifices *there is a remembrance made of sins year by year. 4 For it is impossible that the blood of bulls and goats should take away sins. 5 Wherefore when he cometh into the world, he saith,*

Sacrifice and offering thou wouldest not,
But a body didst thou prepare for me;

6 In whole burnt offerings and sacrifices *for sin thou hadst no pleasure:*

7 Then said I, Lo, I am come
   (In the roll of the book it is written of me)
   To do thy will, O God.
8 Saying above, Sacrifices and offerings and whole burnt
offerings and sacrifices for sin thou wouldest not, neither
hadst pleasure therein (the which are offered according to
the law), 9 then hath he said, Lo, I am come to do thy will.
He taketh away the first, that he may establish the second.
10 By which will we have been sanctified through the offering of the body of Jesus Christ once for all. 11 And every
priest indeed standeth day by day ministering and offering
oftentimes the same sacrifices, the which can never take
away sins: 12 but he, when he had offered one sacrifice for
sins for ever, sat down on the right hand of God; 13
henceforth expecting till his enemies be made the footstool
of his feet. 14 For by one offering he hath perfected for
ever them that are sanctified. 15 And the Holy Spirit also
beareth witness to us; for after he hath said,

16 This is the covenant that I will make with them
    After those days, saith the Lord:
    I will put my laws on their heart,
    And upon their mind also will I write them;
then saith he,
17 And their sins and their iniquities will I remember no
    more.
18 Now where remission of these is, there is no more offer-
    ing for sin.

Here the writer reaches his great climax. He brings to
a conclusion his contrast between the Levitical priesthood
and the priesthood of Christ. He has shown that the latter
was in a better scene, not in an earthly tabernacle but in
the sphere of heavenly realities. (Ch. 8:1-6.) It was under better conditions, related to a covenant of grace rather
than one of works. (Vs. 7-13.) He has then compared
the redeeming work of Christ with the ritual of the Day of
Atonement. On that day, in virtue of sacrifices offered,
the high priest could enter the Holy of Holies. He must be
alone. He might enter only once a year. The very ritual
thus indicated that full, free access to God was not yet
made possible. Such access has been secured by the en-

trance of Christ into the heavenly sanctuary.   (Ch. 9.)

The sacrifice of Christ, unlike the sacrifice of the old ritual, was abiding in its efficacy.   It need not be repeated. This already has been stated.   (Vs. 25-26.)

The idea is now expanded, and the truth is established by quotations from the Old Testament.   The Jewish sacrificial system dealt only with types of the true spiritual realities.   It could not, by its repeated offerings, secure the complete salvation of those who took part in its rites. "For the law having a shadow of the good things to come, not the very image of the things, can never with the same sacrifices year by year, which they offer continually, make perfect them that draw nigh."   These sacrifices could not give peace of conscience, or bring the worshipers into an ideal relationship with God.   (Ch. 10:1.)

The very repetition of these sacrifices was a proof that the ancient ritual could not effect the atonement of which it was a shadow.   Otherwise would these sacrifices "not have ceased to be offered"?   The fact that every year, on the Day of Atonement, confession of sins was renewed, shows that the effect of these sacrifices was temporary and that the people had not been granted a real sense of forgiveness.   This was inevitable: "For it is impossible that the blood of bulls and goats should take away sins."   (Vs. 2-4.)

This inadequacy of animal sacrifices made necessary a new offering, namely, the self-sacrifice of Christ.   A portion of Psalm 40 is quoted in vs. 5-7 to express Christ's own conception of his divine mission.   He came into the world fully conscious that the Levitical offerings were quite inadequate as means of atonement.   He came to do the will of God, not merely by a life of moral perfection, but by offering himself as a divine sacrifice for sin.   He realized that the redeeming will of God necessitated his own atoning death.

The psalmist probably meant simply that moral obedience is better than material sacrifices.   The author, however, uses the words of the psalmist to set forth the truth that the self-sacrifice of Christ, in submission to the will of God, is far better than all "burnt offerings and sacrifices for sin." The conclusion, therefore, is reached that the Mosaic sacrifices have been superseded by the sacrifice of Christ: "He taketh away the first, that he may establish the second." Furthermore, the divine will was fulfilled, in accordance with which Christ yielded himself to a sacrificial death, and the purpose of God was accomplished in that men were brought into true fellowship with God: "By which will we have been sanctified through the offering of the body of Jesus Christ once for all." (Vs. 5-10.)

The sacrifice of Christ is also final. Note how it is contrasted with the ministry of the Levitical priests. The latter were seen standing and repeating the same offerings again and again. Christ offered himself once for all; and the finality of his work is evident from the fact that he no longer stands ministering but is now seated in the place of supreme power. "For by one offering he hath perfected for ever them that are sanctified." Nothing further remains to be done. By the one sacrifice Christ has provided cleansing of conscience and has opened a way whereby men can be brought into continuing fellowship with God. (Vs. 11-14.)

To establish this fact the writer, who has quoted from the Law and from The Psalms, now again reverts to the prophecy in which mention was made of the new covenant and in which there was a prediction of final pardon (Jer. 31:33-34). He refers to the spiritual nature of this covenant, and mentions forgiveness and moral renewal as its chief characteristics. Therefore he concludes that where these results have been attained there can be no further need of sacrifices, for "where remission of these [iniquities] is, there is no more offering for sin." (Heb. 10:15-18.)

Thus the author argues for the abiding efficacy of the work of Christ, and also for the absolute finality of the Christian faith.

II
PRACTICAL: THE LIFE
OF BELIEVERS
Chs. 10:19 to 13:17

A. THE PRIVILEGES OF THE CHRISTIAN LIFE
Chs. 10:19-25

19 Having therefore, brethren, boldness to enter into the holy place by the blood of Jesus, 20 by the way which he dedicated for us, a new and living way, through the veil, that is to say, his flesh; 21 and having a great priest over the house of God; 22 let us draw near with a true heart in fulness of faith, having our hearts sprinkled from an evil conscience: and having our body washed with pure water, 23 let us hold fast the confession of our hope that it waver not; for he is faithful that promised: 24 and let us consider one another to provoke unto love and good works; 25 not forsaking our own assembling together, as the custom of some is, but exhorting one another; and so much the more, as ye see the day drawing nigh.

The New Testament epistles commonly consist of two parts. One is doctrinal and the other practical. The first sets forth Christian truth; the second applies the truth to life. This analysis is not exact, for both parts usually contain instruction; both include exhortation. It is helpful, however, to mark such general divisions and to note their separate contents.

Thus, in The Epistle to the Hebrews, the opening chapters present the atoning work of Christ under the types of the Old Testament priesthood. The closing chapters enjoin upon the readers conduct becoming those who have accepted the salvation provided by Christ. The first part does contain impressive exhortations and warnings. These, however, are rather parenthetic, while in the second part they form the very substance of the message. They are based upon the privileges of the Christian life; they concern its trials and temptations and they enforce its social and religious duties.

However, care must be taken lest the two parts of the epistle be too far separated. They are vitally related. Thus the first exhortation of this "practical" section is immediately connected with the truth previously established. The writer has shown that Christ has secured for his followers immediate and free access to God, that the former religious system has been done away, and that a new covenant has been established. Now he enjoins a better life. The two sections are linked together by the word "therefore." In view of what Christ has done, the readers are encouraged to accept their privileges and to fulfill their duties.

The paragraph consists of a single sentence: "Having therefore, brethren, boldness to enter into the holy place . . . and having a great priest . . . let us draw near . . . in . . . faith, . . . let us hold fast . . . our hope . . . and let us consider one another to provoke unto love." Thus the threefold exhortation is based upon two facts which the previous portion of the epistle has established, namely, the access to God which has been secured and the continuing power of Christ. This access is described as "boldness to enter into the holy place," into the divine presence, a privilege enjoyed under the ancient ritual by the high priest alone and by him only once a year. This privilege now belongs to every believer. It has been secured "by the blood of Jesus." It is a "new" way, one which, after a long period of preparation and prophecy, Christ has inaugurated or "dedicated." It is a "living way," for perfect fellowship with God is made possible by a living Christ, in contrast with the blood of the dead sacrifices of the ancient religious system. Yet it was made possible by his death. This fact, so often repeated, is presented here by a striking figure. The way of access which Christ has opened is "through the veil, that is to say, his flesh." In the tabernacle, a veil shut out all worshipers from the Holy of Holies. The crucifixion of Christ was like the rending of that veil. The barrier was removed. By virtue of his sacrifice, by means of his atoning work, all who trust in him can enjoy immediate and confident entrance into the holy place, to the mercy seat, to the throne of grace, to a loving God.

A second privilege is mentioned, "having a great priest over the house of God." By "the house of God" the writer must mean that sphere of divine realities in which Christ serves in contrast with the shadows and types of the Jewish ritual; but it must also denote the people of God for whom Christ ministers. The blessed assurance is of a Redeemer who is in the place of authority and is abundantly able to save those who come unto God by him.

In view of such privileges the writer makes his appeal, "Let us draw near with a true heart in fulness of faith." Approach to God requires sincerity and confidence. We come as those whose hearts have been "sprinkled from an evil conscience" and whose bodies have been "washed with pure water." The reference is to the Mosaic ritual. According to its requirements, the priests who were to minister in the tabernacle must be sprinkled with the blood of sacrifices and bathed in water from the brazen laver. The Christian worshiper is one whose conscience has been given peace and whose inner life has been purified by the blood of Christ. The outer life also has been cleansed. The body has been "washed with pure water." The truth which the Spirit of Christ applies to the believer effects such cleansing; and of this the water of baptism is the symbol. We are not asked to have "our hearts sprinkled" and to be "washed" in order that we may approach God; but rather in view of what Christ has done for us by his atoning death and by his transforming power we are urged to draw near to God in the full assurance, or the "fulness," of faith.

Furthermore, since the immediate presence of God has been made accessible to us, and since Christ now ministers as Priest in our behalf, "Let us hold fast the confession of our hope that it waver not." The content of this hope is the perfect blessedness, the completed salvation, the heavenly vision, which await us in the "better country." This confident expectation Christians must hold in the face of all mysteries, all discouragements, all doubts, all ridicule, all unbelief. They are urged to do so on the best of grounds: "For he is faithful that promised." The promise of God cannot fail of fulfillment. In spite of clouds and darkness our faces should be turned toward the morning and our hearts should be full of glad expectation as we look toward that future glory which is to be shared by those who trust and love Christ.

There is a third virtue which should characterize the people of the great High Priest. They should draw near in faith, they should hold and profess their hope, but they should manifest their "love." This should be shown first of all toward their fellow believers. "Let us consider one another," or "let us bestow thought upon one another." Let this be with a view "to provoke unto love and good works," that is, to promote in one another the spirit of brotherhood and right conduct, to incite, to arouse, to stimulate such a spirit.

With this in view, we should be regular in our attendance upon the services of the church, "not forsaking our own assembling together, as the custom of some is." These meetings of the Christian brotherhood were evidently for mutual help, for encouraging or "exhorting one another." What led some to neglect these gatherings, the writer does not state. Probably the causes would have a familiar sound to Christians of today should they all have been enumerated. Less familiar is the reason given for faithful attendance at the place of worship, "and so much the more, as ye see the day drawing nigh." The day is that of our

Lord's return.   The signs of that return which those readers might have been able to "see," one can hardly conjecture.   Surely such a united hope and expectation should
make Christian fellowship and social worship more helpful
and more precious.

When Christ comes, faith and hope and love will all continue; but "the greatest of these is love," and it will find its
glorious consummation in the perfect fellowship of "the
saints in light."

B. A WARNING AGAINST WILLFUL SIN
Ch. 10:26-31

*26 For if we sin wilfully after that we have received the
knowledge of the truth, there remaineth no more a sacrifice
for sins, 27 but a certain fearful expectation of judgment,
and a fierceness of fire which shall devour the adversaries.
28 A man that hath set at nought Moses' law dieth without
compassion on the word of two or three witnesses: 29 of
how much sorer punishment, think ye, shall he be judged
worthy, who hath trodden under foot the Son of God, and
hath counted the blood of the covenant wherewith he was
sanctified an unholy thing, and hath done despite unto the
Spirit of grace?   30 For we know him that said, Vengeance
belongeth unto me, I will recompense.   And again, The
Lord shall judge his people.   31 It is a fearful thing to fall
into the hands of the living God.*

There are two phases of the return of Christ.   One is
associated with hope, the other with wrath.   The first secures deliverance and blessedness for the followers of
Christ.   The second brings judgment upon his enemies.
The author has made reference to the former phase to encourage his readers in faithful attendance upon the meetings for common worship.   He uses the punitive phase to
give solemn sanction to his warning against willful sin.

This willful sin seems to be closely associated in the
mind of the writer with the holding aloof from Christian

gatherings. "Not forsaking our own assembling together" (v. 25) and "for if we sin wilfully" (v. 26) seem to be related clauses. The neglect of Christian fellowship and worship seemed to imply a disregard of Christianity and even a rejection of it as the full and final revelation of God. Such a course could only result in hopeless ruin for the offender in the approaching "day" of the Lord's return.

Surely, to "sin wilfully" means more than yielding to some temptation or being betrayed into some wrong course of action. For such offenses, where there is true repentance, pardon can be assured. The sinful course here described is deliberate, presumptuous, insistent. It is equivalent to a denial of Christ and to the abandonment of Christianity. It denotes actual and avowed apostasy. Upon such apostates judgment must surely fall. "For if we sin wilfully after that we have received the knowledge of the truth, there remaineth no more a sacrifice for sins, but a certain fearful expectation of judgment, and a fierceness of fire which shall devour the adversaries."

Those described are such as have received and have rejected the full knowledge of the salvation provided by Christ. For them there is no escape. There remains no other availing sacrifice. What does remain is a certain awful "expectation of judgment." The very indefiniteness of the expectation heightens its terror. The writer adds, however, that the retribution will issue from a fiery indignation which will destroy the enemies of God.

The certainty of such judgment is established by a reference to the law of Moses, and then by two quotations from the Old Testament. The argument, based on the Mosaic law, is "from the less to the greater." If the penalty for willful sin, for rejecting the old covenant, for blaspheming God, was severe, how much more severe is the judgment which should be expected by one who rejects the salvation of Christ? According to the ancient code, apostasy, when attested by two or three witnesses, was summarily punished by the penalty of death; "of how much sorer punishment, think ye, shall he be judged worthy" who disregards and despises the grace and mercy and love revealed in Christ!

The guilt of such an offender is detailed in three particulars. He has "trodden under foot the Son of God." He has treated with scorn and insult the highest and best of all beings; he has trampled upon the only begotten Son of God.

He has "counted the blood of the covenant wherewith he was sanctified an unholy thing." The blood of Christ is the instrument by which men are cleansed from sin and made fit for fellowship with God and for his service, and thus are made to share in the blessings of the new covenant. This "blood" the apostate regards and treats as something common and unclean.

In the third place, he has "done despite unto the Spirit of grace." He has insulted the Holy Spirit and despised his work. By this Spirit we have access to God, we are given assurance of his presence and love, and are granted gifts for his service. The apostate is guilty of blaspheming the very Agent by whom the grace of God is communicated to man.

The certainty of punishment is emphasized by two quotations from Deuteronomy, both of which are attributed to God: "For we know him that said, Vengeance belongeth unto me, I will recompense. And again, The Lord shall judge his people" (Heb. 10:30).

The first of these quotations emphasizes the fact that the divine judgment will be a strict and exact requital. The very dreadfulness of the doom lies in the fact that by it absolute justice will be done.

The second quotation, like the first, was used in the Old Testament in the sense that God would exercise his protecting care over his people, just as the first meant that he would punish their enemies. Here, however, both quotations are best understood as declarations of judgment, the first of its justice, the second of its extent. It will include all who have been known as the people of God. Outward profession, or peculiar privilege, will not exempt one from judgment; they may only increase the severity of inevitable doom.

Thus the writer solemnly concludes, "It is a fearful thing to fall into the hands of the living God." It is absolute folly to defy moral law, or to disregard the moral order which inexorably punishes all by whom it is flouted or disobeyed. More terrible still is the madness of willfully meriting the retribution of "the living God," and of treating with contempt his gracious provision for pardon and peace and eternal joy.

C. THE PRINCIPLE OF THE CHRISTIAN LIFE
Chs. 10:32 to 12:2

1. THE EXPERIENCE OF FAITH Ch. 10:32-39

32 But call to remembrance the former days, in which, after ye were enlightened, ye endured a great conflict of sufferings; 33 partly, being made a gazingstock both by reproaches and afflictions; and partly, becoming partakers with them that were so used. 34 For ye both had compassion on them that were in bonds, and took joyfully the spoiling of your possessions, knowing that ye have for yourselves a better possession and an abiding one. 35 Cast not away therefore your boldness, which hath great recompense of reward. 36 For ye have need of patience, that, having done the will of God, ye may receive the promise. 37 For yet a very little while,
He that cometh shall come, and shall not tarry.
38 But my righteous one shall live by faith:
And if he shrink back, my soul hath no pleasure in him.
39 But we are not of them that shrink back unto perdition; but of them that have faith unto the saving of the soul.

The author began the practical portion of his epistle with an exhortation (ch. 10:19-25), which was followed by a warning (vs. 26-31). Now the warning gives place to a message of encouragement. (Vs. 32-39.) Both the exhortation and the warning were enforced by reference to the return of Christ. In view of that same event the readers are urged to continue to "live by faith." The coming of Christ may be near, and he will bring to believers the fulfillment of their hopes and will deliver them from their enemies.

They have been warned against the peril of apostasy. They are now assured that such will not be their fate. Their previous experience is recalled. The appeal to memory gives strength for present trials. The noble record of the past is a summons to defend the laurels already won; and the final reward is near.

The entire paragraph is an encouragement to unwavering confidence in the promises of God. Faith is the supreme and formative principle of the Christian life. In the chapter which follows, its power will be illustrated by the lives of great Hebrew heroes. By the readers something of this power has already been experienced. In their earlier days, by their faith in God, they had triumphed over persecution and had been made willing to suffer with fellow Christians who were in distress.

"Call to remembrance the former days," is the plea. Memory is one of life's chief comforters. Therefore recall those early experiences which followed soon after you had received a saving knowledge of Christ. "Ye endured a great conflict of sufferings." Through this conflict they passed in triumph. The sufferings were of two kinds. Part of them were endured in their own persons. Part were due to their sympathy and to their voluntary sharing with the distress of others. They themselves had been "made a gazingstock both by reproaches and afflictions." They had become a public spectacle, amid reproaches and persecutions, derided, denounced, unjustly suspected, falsely accused.

All this they had endured bravely. Nor were they indifferent to the sufferings of their fellow Christians. They became "partakers with them that were so used," and "had compassion on them that were in bonds."

Their own personal losses, whether due to confiscation or plunder of their goods, they had met not only with patience but actually with joy. All this, faith had made possible. It had made them confident that in heaven they had "a better possession and an abiding one."

These memories are now pressed home. "Cast not away therefore your boldness, which hath great recompense of reward." Your confidence must be retained. It is the condition of receiving a great reward. Patience is needed, "that, having done the will of God, ye may receive" the fulfillment of "the promise." This will of God may include suffering, and practical sympathy, and hopeful waiting. Whatever it involves, the believer who submits to it, who trustfully obeys it, will receive all that God has promised. And this promise is soon to be fulfilled. The time now is not long:

> "For yet a very little while,
> He that cometh shall come, and shall not tarry.
> But my righteous ones shall live by faith:
> And if he shrink back, my soul hath no pleasure
>   in him."

With certain changes, the writer quotes the familiar words of the ancient prophet (Hab. 2:3-4) in order to enforce his teaching. He uses the phrases with a somewhat altered meaning; but they convey with a certain solemn emphasis the truth he wishes to enforce. The return of Christ should ever be regarded as near. The just man, the true follower of Christ, can only live, and maintain his patience and courage and hope, by the exercise of faith. One who draws back, who becomes an apostate, who ceases to trust in God, is subject to the displeasure of God.

Therefore, the author triumphantly concludes: "We are not of them that shrink back unto perdition; but of them that have faith unto the saving of the soul."

2. THE ILLUSTRATIONS OF FAITH   Chs. 11:1 to 12:2

a. The Nature of Faith   Ch. 11:1-3

1 Now faith is assurance of things hoped for, a conviction of things not seen. 2 For therein the elders had witness borne to them. 3 By faith we understand that the worlds have been framed by the word of God, so that what is seen hath not been made out of things which appear.

The readers have been encouraged to continue steadfast in faith. This has been done by calling to mind their own experience of the power of faith, and by the assurance that the promises of God are certain to be fulfilled. (Ch. 10:32-39.)

Further encouragement is now given by reviewing the triumphs of faith in the lives of Hebrew heroes and, supremely, by pointing to the example of Jesus. (Chs. 11:1 to 12:2.)

Before he summons this great "cloud of witnesses" the writer gives a brief introduction, stating the nature of faith, its power in human lives, and its solution of the problem of the world's origin. (Ch. 11:1-3.)

In setting forth the nature of faith the author does not attempt an abstract definition. In fact, he is more concerned with what faith does than with what faith is. However, his previous references to faith indicate that he means by it trust in the promises of God. Here it is described as a firm confidence that what is hoped for will come to pass, an assured "conviction" of the existence of invisible realities. Yet it is implied that this confidence and this conviction are based on revelations which God has made. In fact, any real definition of faith must include the idea of a divine revelation. Otherwise what is called faith may be mere credulity or conjecture. Faith is "taking God at his word." Faith is "accepting as true what God has revealed." It is "man's genuine answer to the realities of divine revelation."

Thus if the writer here describes faith as "assurance of things hoped for," he would have it understood that this "assurance" rests on divine promises. If faith is "a conviction of things not seen," it is implied that this "conviction" relates to realities which God has brought to light.

Furthermore, to the writer faith is something intensely practical. It is not sentiment or mere speculation. It is always expressed in life. Faith accepts what God has revealed, and then acts, with the absolute confidence that the revelation is true. Thus the author treats it as "an active conviction which moves and molds human conduct."

Therefore he at once adds, "For therein the elders had witness borne to them." This is the theme of the entire chapter. It shows, by a series of illustrations, the influence of faith upon life. "The elders" denote all those of former years who put their trust in God. Faith is no novelty in the religious experience of the race. It was because of their faith that men of old time "had witness borne to them." It was this principle of life for which the Old Testament saints were distinguished. Because of their trust in him, they won the approval of God, and they have been immortalized in Scripture.

Faith is chiefly concerned with the future. It rests on the promises of God and confidently awaits blessings which are to come. Yet it is related also to unseen realities whether of the future, the present, or the past.

For this reason the author begins his long list of illustrations with the statement, "By faith we understand that the worlds have been framed by the word of God, so that what is seen hath not been made out of things which appear." Our belief in the origin of the universe is a supreme example of "a conviction of things not seen." It is an act of faith, and faith is "accepting what God has revealed." The visible worlds point to an invisible Creator.

> "The heavens declare the glory of God;
> And the firmament showeth his handiwork."

Faith gives us an assured conviction that the visible order as a whole cannot be traced to physical causes. It has been constituted by a divine fiat or command, "by the word of God." It is an expression of the divine will. It has "not been made out of things which appear." "Material causation" cannot explain the origin of the world. The theory of evolution may deal with processes; it has no satisfying word as to origins. The first line of Scripture is an arresting expression of faith: "In the beginning God created the heavens and the earth."

b. The Faith of Abel, Enoch, and Noah   Ch. 11:4-7

4 By faith Abel offered unto God a more excellent sacrifice than Cain, through which he had witness borne to him that he was righteous, God bearing witness in respect of his gifts: and through it he being dead yet speaketh. 5 By faith Enoch was translated that he should not see death; and he was not found, because God translated him: for he hath had witness borne to him that before his translation he had been well-pleasing unto God: 6 and without faith it is impossible to be well-pleasing unto him; for he that cometh to God must believe that he is, and that he is a rewarder of them that seek after him. 7 By faith Noah, being warned of God concerning things not seen as yet, moved with godly fear, prepared an ark to the saving of his house; through which he condemned the world, and became heir of the righteousness which is according to faith.

The first exercise of faith to which the writer refers is that which accepts the fact of creation, according to which "the worlds have been framed by the word of God." The second is that which enables men to live in right relations to God. It is illustrated from the lives of three men who, before the days of Abraham, stand out prominently, in the narrative of Genesis, as heroes of faith. These three are Abel, Enoch, and Noah. The exact aspect of faith, of which each was an example, has been variously understood. Possibly they may be taken severally as showing the faith of one who is worshiping God, of one who is walking with God, and of one who is witnessing for God.

One of these men was murdered; the second never died; the third preserved the life of the human race. Abel may be a picture of the true worshiper. The altar he erected at the gates of Eden, and his smoking sacrifice, may typify those places and means by which, through the passing ages, men have sought access to God. Just how God had revealed himself to Abel, and how he had made known his will, we do not know. Nor are we told in what way he showed his acceptance of the offering of Abel and his displeasure with the offering of Cain. It was "by faith," by taking God at his word, by obedience to him, that "Abel offered unto God a more excellent sacrifice than Cain." There is a right and there is a wrong way of approach if one would worship God. There is a perfect Sacrifice, there is "a new and living way," of which the whole of The Epistle to the Hebrews has been speaking. There is a Lamb which was offered "from the foundation of the world." In virtue of his atoning death, one may with confidence "draw nigh to God." All the sacrifices made since paradise was lost are but shadows "of the Lamb that hath been slain," to whom all praise and glory will be given when paradise is regained. We are to present no offering of our own devising, but to trust in the merits of "the Lamb of God, that taketh away the sin of the world."

Thus, prompted by faith, Abel offered his "more excellent sacrifice," and obtained from God the testimony "that he was righteous." Thus, too, by faith, manifested in his offering, "he being dead yet speaketh." His witness is living. He by that first recorded act of worship still testifies that one who is to worship God acceptably must come in faith, presenting the offering which God requires and expecting the pardon and peace which God provides.

"By faith Enoch was translated that he should not see death." This then is the New Testament explantion of what is meant by the words of Genesis: "He was not; for God took him." Vital, breathing, painless, he was transformed, transfigured, and without passing through the dark portals of death was caught away to enter the larger life and the joys of heaven. This is regarded by the writer of the epistle as the natural issue of an earthly career which is described by saying that "he had been well-pleasing unto God," or in the Old Testament phrase he had "walked with God." As a saintly commentator remarked, "Enoch walked with God and one day he walked so far that he never came back again." Walking with God implies fellowship and agreement. Two cannot walk together unless they are moving in the same direction. This agreement, this fellowship, implies faith; thus the writer adds, "And without faith it is impossible to be well-pleasing unto him; for he that cometh to God must believe that he is, and that he is a rewarder of them that seek after him." To believe, not only in the existence of God, but in his sovereign and moral rule, and to live in accordance with such a belief— this makes it possible to walk with God, to please God, to enjoy his fellowship, and finally to enter upon his glory either by the gateway of death or, if living until Christ returns, by being "caught up in the clouds, to meet the Lord in the air," to "ever be with the Lord."

The faith of Noah (v. 7) is an illustration of "a conviction of things not seen," and it further indicates that faith is a response to a divine revelation. Still further it shows that faith enables one to witness for God. Noah was "a preacher of righteousness." To him God revealed the fact of an approaching deluge. He was "warned of God concerning things not seen as yet." So, taking God at his word, with due reverence for his command, he "prepared an ark to the saving of his house." Far away from the sea, with no sign of a flood, he built the strange craft. This act of faith "condemned" the unbelieving, scoffing world which refused to accept the warning of the prophet. Furthermore, by it he came to possess, he became entitled to, he "became heir of the righteousness which is according to faith."

An unbelieving world has always been slow to accept

the warnings of God and has been skeptical of his way of salvation. Yet God has never left men without witnesses whose faith has rebuked unbelief and secured the righteousness in which faith results.

c. The Faith of the Patriarchs   Ch. 11:8-22

8 By faith Abraham, when he was called, obeyed to go out unto a place which he was to receive for an inheritance; and he went out, not knowing whither he went. 9 By faith he became a sojourner in the land of promise, as in a land not his own, dwelling in tents, with Isaac and Jacob, the heirs with him of the same promise: 10 for he looked for the city which hath the foundations, whose builder and maker is God. 11 By faith even Sarah herself received power to conceive seed when she was past age, since she counted him faithful who had promised: 12 wherefore also there sprang of one, and him as good as dead, so many as the stars of heaven in multitude, and as the sand, which is by the sea-shore, innumerable.

13 These all died in faith, not having received the promises, but having seen them and greeted them from afar, and having confessed that they were strangers and pilgrims on the earth. 14 For they that say such things make it manifest that they are seeking after a country of their own. 15 And if indeed they had been mindful of that country from which they went out, they would have had opportunity to return. 16 But now they desire a better country, that is, a heavenly: wherefore God is not ashamed of them, to be called their God; for he hath prepared for them a city.

17 By faith Abraham, being tried, offered up Isaac: yea, he that had gladly received the promises was offering up his only begotten son; 18 even he to whom it was said, In Isaac shall thy seed be called: 19 accounting that God is able to raise up, even from the dead; from whence he did also in a figure receive him back. 20 By faith Isaac blessed Jacob and Esau, even concerning things to come. 21 By faith Jacob, when he was dying, blessed each of the sons of Joseph; and worshipped, leaning upon the top of his staff. 22 By faith Joseph, when his end was nigh, made mention of the departure of the children of Israel; and gave commandment concerning his bones.

It is natural that in a roll of the heroes of faith the supreme place should be assigned to Abraham. He is known as the "Father of the Faithful" and in him, of all the Old Testament saints, the power of faith is most perfectly set forth. With his name are united those of Sarah and Isaac and Jacob and Joseph; but the largest space is devoted to the first and greatest of the patriarchs.

As narrated by the writer, his life is summarized in four great manifestations of faith: he obeyed God; he sojourned in the Land of Promise; he obtained the blessing; he offered his son as a sacrifice. First of all, then, "By faith Abraham, when he was called, obeyed to go out unto a place which he was to receive for an inheritance." Two difficulties were involved. Much that was precious in life must be left behind; there was mystery in the experience which lay ahead. The latter is emphasized by the author: "He went out, not knowing whither he went." It is so in all the great crises of human life, in beginning to follow Christ, in undertaking each new task. Something must be given up; yet the difficulty is in the uncertainty of what lies before.

By faith Abraham plunged into a desert; by faith he obeyed. Faith is a response to the promises of God. To Abraham he had said that he would bless him and make him a blessing. Abraham believed God and set forth on his journey. So it is in entering the Christian life, so in attempting a new, great work. When God gives the assurance of blessings to be received and to be conferred, faith obeys and steps forth, not knowing whither God may lead.

"By faith he became a sojourner in the land of promise, as in a land not his own." That is surprising. He lived in his own land as in a land which belonged to another. Why? "He looked for the city which hath the foundations,

whose builder and maker is God." He expected to see
God's rule, God's Kingdom, God's city established on
earth. Indeed, his longings and hopes would not be satisfied until he entered the heavenly city on high. So he lived
as a pilgrim and a stranger. For this reason he built no
home. He dwelt "in tents, with Isaac and Jacob, the heirs
with him of the same promise." Such dwellings were the
very symbols of that which is temporary and transient.

So the pilgrim life is lived today. Faith believes in the
promise of a heavenly city in the light of which the nations
of the world are yet to walk. Faith seeks to hasten the descent of that city upon earth. Faith regards that city as the
rightful home. So faith does not consider the accidents of
life as of supreme importance. It does not try to build
permanent abiding places while waiting and working for
the city of God. The tent may be costly or poor. The
surroundings may be lovely or forlorn. While his heart is
set upon the coming of that city, a man can be satisfied and
not too far concerned with the things which are temporal.
He is expecting a permanent place in the order which will
be eternal.

By faith the promise to Abraham of a son was fulfilled.
To him was born a child in whom all the nations of the
world were to be blessed. Here, however, it is the faith
not of Abraham, but of Sarah, his wife, that is mentioned.
This is the more surprising since in the Old Testament
story nothing is said of her faith but only of her incredulity
and unbelief. It may be concluded that Abraham communicated his faith to Sarah. When they were united in their
faith the blessing came and "there sprang of one, and him
as good as dead, so many as the stars of heaven in multitude, and as the sand, which is by the sea-shore, innumerable." Thus, immeasurable blessings have ever come from
homes in which husband and wife have been one in their
belief and hope.

The complete fulfillment of the promises was not received, however, by Abraham and Sarah, nor by Isaac and

Jacob. "These all died in faith, not having received the promises, but having seen them and greeted them from afar, and having confessed that they were strangers and pilgrims on the earth." Before the Redeemer had come, while the Land of Promise was under the sway of heathen cruelty and sin, these patriarchs could not regard the country as their own. Their country was not the land they had left, nor was it Canaan, to which they had come. Their desire was for "a better country, that is, a heavenly." Until they came to heaven or heaven came to earth they could not be at home. In view of such longings and desires God recognized them as his own people. He is "not ashamed . . . to be called their God." He will yet fulfill their high hopes, "for he hath prepared for them a city."

The supreme proof of the faith of Abraham was when, "being tried," he "offered up Isaac." The severity of the trial was not that it brought a father's love into conflict with a divine command. The real difficulty lay in the apparent conflict between the promise of God and the command of God. If all nations were to be blessed in Isaac, how could God require that Isaac should be sacrificed? Here faith won its supreme victory. Faith believed that the blessing would come, even though Isaac should be slain. Yet how could this be? Only by having Isaac raised from the dead. Thus faith invented the truth of resurrection, "accounting that God is able to raise up, even from the dead." It was "from the dead," figuratively speaking, that Abraham did receive back his son. Isaac had been given up by his father. In all reality his life had been offered, when by an act of God he was rescued, and raised up, and restored.

So faith ever reconciles the love of God with the mysterious providences of God. To solve the problem it introduces the factors of resurrection and immortality. It rests confident that in the light of eternity we shall understand the riddles of time.

With Abraham the writer associates Isaac and Jacob and Joseph. These patriarchs may be regarded as illustrating the farsightedness of faith. Out of their long and dramatic careers are selected only those scenes with which their lives were closed. In a very real sense "these all died in faith." Isaac, aged and weak and physically blind, saw clearly with the eye of faith. He beheld the future and the relative greatness of his two sons. He "blessed Jacob and Esau, even concerning things to come."

Jacob in his clouded day passed through tempest and through storm; but at even time there was light. He saw his son standing next to the throne of Egypt, and looking by faith into the mysterious future he pronounced a distinct and distinguishing blessing on each of the two sons of Joseph. He did so by faith, believing that God would fulfill his promises of goodness and glory through those sons. He "worshipped," in his infirmity, "leaning upon the top of his staff."

"By faith Joseph, when his end was nigh," saw clearly through the mists of about four hundred years. He "made mention of the departure of the children of Israel" from Egypt. He "gave commandment concerning his bones." He knew that God would fulfill his promise and would bring his people to the Land of Canaan. His body might be embalmed and laid in a royal tomb. Centuries might pass. Yet in the time which God had predicted, the people of God would leave the land of bondage. So Joseph exacted a promise that his bones should not be left in Egypt but should be brought to the Promised Land and there be buried where the bodies of Abraham and Isaac and Jacob had been laid to rest. So faith ever looks across the unknown years which lie between, and sees the delights of the land of far distances, the abiding home of the people of God.

d. The Faith of Moses and of Israel   Ch. 11:23-31

23 By faith Moses, when he was born, was hid three months by his parents, because they saw he was a goodly

child; and they were not afraid of the king's command-ment. 24 By faith Moses, when he was grown up, refused to be called the son of Pharaoh's daughter; 25 choosing rather to share ill treatment with the people of God, than to enjoy the pleasures of sin for a season; 26 accounting the reproach of Christ greater riches than the treasures of Egypt: for he looked unto the recompense of reward. 27 By faith he forsook Egypt, not fearing the wrath of the king: for he endured, as seeing him who is invisible. 28 By faith he kept the passover, and the sprinkling of the blood, that the destroyer of the firstborn should not touch them. 29 By faith they passed through the Red sea as by dry land: which the Egyptians assaying to do were swal-lowed up. 30 By faith the walls of Jericho fell down, after they had been compassed about for seven days. 31 By faith Rahab the harlot perished not with them that were disobedient, having received the spies with peace.

It is not at all strange that the story of Moses' faith begins with mention of the faith of his parents. Usually the great heroes of faith have come from godly homes. Moses is an example of one of those whose glorious careers can be traced to the piety of their parents. In his case, however, something even more startling is recorded. Here the appearance of the child seems to have quickened the parents' faith. The very order of the words fastens the thought at once upon Moses. We read, "By faith Moses, when he was born, was hid three months by his parents, because they saw he was a goodly child." Very often, it is true, the coming of a little babe into a home awakens in parents thoughts of God and is the occasion of a new religious experience. With the parents of Moses some-thing far more surprising was involved. Their faith was not merely an expectation of his future usefulness based upon the beauty of the child, but the unusual loveliness of that babe made the parents believe that in him a divine promise would be fulfilled. God had foretold that de-liverance was to come for his enslaved people. Centuries earlier he had declared to Abraham definitely that the bondage of Israel was to end after "four hundred years" (Gen. 15:13). Those years had passed. The parents of Moses believed God. Their faith rested upon his promise. It was so strong that it overcame their natural dread of Pharoah's decree that all male infants should be put to death. It led them to conceal the babe. It was rewarded by the rescue of the child and his adoption by the daughter of the king. (Ex., ch. 2.) In this same way the faith of modern parents lays hold upon the promises of God and issues in blessings which eternity cannot bound.

As an infant Moses had stimulated faith; as a man he was impelled by it. Faith determined his heroic and dramatic choice. "But faith Moses, when he was grown up, refused to be called the son of Pharaoh's daughter; choosing rather to share ill treatment with the people of God, than to enjoy the pleasures of sin for a season." His faith appeared in his regarding a race of slaves as the chosen "people of God" and in his believing the divine promises of release and future blessing to the world. This led him to choose to share their humiliation and distress rather than to enjoy for a time "the pleasures of sin." The latter does not refer to possible sensual and unlawful gratifications, but to the continued acceptance of royal favor and all the delights of princely position and power, instead of serving as the deliverer of Israel. The "sin" would have been that of being disloyal to his people and untrue to his divinely appointed task.

"By faith" he made such a choice "accounting the reproach of Christ greater riches than the treasures of Egypt." The reproach he endured was involved in his believing and acting upon the promises of God which found their ultimate fulfillment in Christ. The readers of this epistle knew well what "the reproach of Christ" meant, and what the writer indicated when he used this phrase to describe the voluntary suffering of Moses, the great deliverer, the type of the Savior who in the fullness of time was to appear.

"By faith" he accepted the promises of God and looked to the future. "He looked unto the recompense of reward," to those deliverances, those compensations, those abiding satisfactions, which in time and in eternity, all who trust and obey God are certain to receive.

"By faith he forsook Egypt." To what incident does the writer refer? Was it to the Exodus, when Moses led Israel out of bondage, or was it to his flight to the land of Midian? It is difficult to decide. It is hardly natural for the writer to mention the Exodus before the reference to the Passover. "Forsook" hardly describes the escape of Israel's hosts. "Not fearing the wrath of the king" is hardly descriptive of the departure of the Israelites which, at the time, the king earnestly desired.

The last quotation, however, is difficult to reconcile with the Old Testament story of the flight to Midian, for this states that "Moses fled from the face of Pharaoh." It is possible that the reference is to the great refusal (v. 24), made without being deterred by the king's certain anger — a refusal and a course of conduct which led to the flight from Egypt and finally to the deliverance of his people. More than a single act seems to be indicated as the writer adds, "For he endured, as seeing him who is invisible." He was not turned aside by the wrath of Pharaoh, for he saw the unseen King. This spiritual vision on the part of Moses is the real explanation of his career; it embodies the essence of this great chapter of the epistle, written to illustrate the power of faith as "a conviction of things not seen."

"By faith he kept," or "instituted," "the passover, and the sprinkling of the blood." This was in direct obedience to the explicit but surprising command of God. To believe that the blood of a lamb sprinkled upon the doorposts of their houses would cause the angel of death to pass over the Israelites, and that on the same night they would be delivered from Egypt, required strong faith on the part of Moses. He took God at his word. Salvation did result, and Moses instituted a festival which for centuries has commemorated escape from death and release from bondage and the birth of a nation. This institution became also a promise of a greater deliverance to be wrought by the sacrifice of the Lamb of God who became the Savior of the world.

The faith of Moses was shared by the people of Israel with whom he is identified. His faith was theirs, and in obedience to God's command they made a great venture (Ex. 14:22) and so "passed through the Red sea" as though they were passing over "dry land" (Heb. 11:29). They did not merely discover a safe path; they accomplished the impossible. Their faith is emphasized by contrast with the audacity and presumption of the Egyptians, who, attempting the same thing, were swallowed up by the sea (Ex. 14:23, 28).

This same faith brought the walls of Jericho crashing to the ground. There was no siege of the city. No visible force was applied. The hosts of Israel, in simple reliance upon the word of God, marched in silence around the stronghold, and on the seventh day, according to the divine promise, the triumph was secured and the way opened for the conquest of Canaan. Thus obstacles in the path of progress are ever being removed for those who put their trust in God.

In connection with this national triumph the faith of one person is mentioned. It is that of a woman who is a strange contrast to Sarah and the mother of Moses, the other women to whom the writer of the epistle has referred. She is a Gentile and an outcast. "By faith Rahab the harlot perished not with them that were disobedient, having received the spies with peace." Her faith was extraordinary. It was founded upon reports brought to her concerning God and his people. These reports were shared by all the citizens of Jericho. They refused to believe and obey and so "perished." She showed her faith by her works (James 2:25), risking her own life to protect the Hebrew spies. "By faith" she was saved and be-

came an ancestress of Jesus and one in the long line
of notorious sinners who "through their faith" have been
redeemed and have "had witness borne to them."

e. "A Cloud of Witnesses"   Ch. 11:32-40

*32 And what shall I more say? for the time will fail me
if I tell of Gideon, Barak, Samson, Jephthah; of David and
Samuel and the prophets: 33 who through faith subdued
kingdoms, wrought righteousness, obtained promises,
stopped the mouths of lions, 34 quenched the power of fire,
escaped the edge of the sword, from weakness were made
strong, waxed mighty in war, turned to flight armies of
aliens. 35 Women received their dead by a resurrection:
and others were tortured, not accepting their deliverance;
that they might obtain a better resurrection: 36 and others
had trial of mockings and scourgings, yea, moreover of
bonds and imprisonment: 37 they were stoned, they were
sawn asunder, they were tempted, they were slain with the
sword: they went about in sheepskins, in goatskins; being
destitute, afflicted, ill-treated 38 (of whom the world was
not worthy), wandering in deserts and mountains and
caves, and the holes of the earth. 39 And these all, having
had witness borne to them through their faith, received not
the promise, 40 God having provided some better thing
concerning us, that apart from us they should not be made
perfect.*

For lack of space and time the writer now summarizes
the achievements of the heroes of subsequent Jewish history. So superb a paragraph should not have its literary
beauty marred by an attempted analysis. Yet the impression may be deepened by noting that reference is made
first to the achievements of these heroes, then to their sufferings, and finally to their rewards. The list includes not
only famous names of Old Testament days, but seems to
include references to the victors and martyrs of the Maccabean age. They "through faith subdued kingdoms,"
as did the Judges and David; "wrought righteousness" in
establishing a just government; "obtained promises," not

those of the coming Messiah, but those of special times
and needs (Josh. 21:45; Judg. 7:7; 13:5; I Kings 8:56);
"stopped the mouths of lions," as in the case of Daniel;
"quenched the power of fire," when the three friends of
Daniel were cast into the flaming furnace; "escaped the
edge of the sword," as David eluded the javelin of Saul,
as Elijah was delivered from Jezebel, or as the entire nation
was saved by the intercession of Esther. "From weakness
were made strong, waxed mighty in war, turned to flight
armies of aliens" may refer to Deborah, to David, to the
Maccabees.

"Women received their dead by a resurrection." At
least two cases are in mind: the widow of Zarephath
(I Kings 17:17-24) and the Shunammite woman (II Kings
4:32-37). This raising of the dead forms a climax to the
achievements of faith and it introduces the tragic list of
the martyrdoms of faith. On their cruel details it is impossible to dwell. The entire history of the Jews is dark-
ened by the records of fiendish tortures inflicted both by
them and upon them. Eleazar and the seven brethren
who died in bitter anguish (II Macc. 6:18-31; ch. 7)
might have escaped had they been willing to recant. They
"were tortured, not accepting their deliverance; that they
might obtain a better resurrection"—not a mere return to
life as in the cases of those at Zarephath and Shunem, but
the entrance upon an immortality of glory.

"Mockings and scourgings" were part of the story just
told; "bonds and imprisonment" were the common experiences of the prophets (I Kings 22:27; Jer. 20:2; 37:15-16;
38:6). "They were stoned," as was Zechariah (II Chron.
24:20-21); "they were sawn asunder," the reputed fate of
Isaiah. "They were tempted" to become apostates by
proffered relief from intolerable torment. "They were
slain with the sword," the experience of Uriah (Jer. 26:23)
and of the fellow prophets of Elijah.

"They went about in sheepskins, in goatskins; being
destitute, afflicted, ill-treated . . . wandering in deserts

and mountains and caves, and the holes of the earth."
Such was true of Elijah and Elisha as well as of the faithful in the Maccabean days.

Surely, of them "the world was not worthy."   They
were treated as though not deserving to live in this world,
whereas really the world was not worthy of their presence.

What was their reward?   For each one it was the recompense of an inviolate conscience, of divine approval, of a
place in the inspired roll of immortals, for "these all . . .
had witness borne to them through their faith."   Yet
they "received not the promise" of all that full blessedness which was to be brought by Christ, "God having
provided some better thing concerning us," namely, that
we should be included with all his people in the privileges
of the "new covenant" and of "the eternal inheritance."
"That apart from us they should not be made perfect"
does not mean that their bliss was dependent upon our
presence or our power, but that their hopes could not be
fulfilled until Christ had wrought out that salvation in
which with them we have a share.

The words are skillfully used to give encouragement to
the readers.   The saints of old triumphed through faith
in promises which they did not see fulfilled.   The readers
live in days which have witnessed the work of the Redeemer.   By the noble example of those less favored
heroes of the past, they should be inspired to endure less
severe trials in expectation of an approaching and complete
reward at the reappearing of Christ.

f. Jesus, the Supreme Example   Ch. 12:1-2

> *1 Therefore let us also, seeing we are compassed about
> with so great a cloud of witnesses, lay aside every weight,
> and the sin which doth so easily beset us, and let us run with
> patience the race that is set before us, 2 looking unto Jesus
> the author and perfecter of our faith, who for the joy that
> was set before him endured the cross, despising shame, and
> hath sat down at the right hand of the throne of God.*

After the long list of ancient heroes, the writer reaches his climax by mentioning Jesus as the unique and matchless illustration of faith. The readers are exhorted to steadfast endurance by heeding the testimony of those heroes, and by fixing their gaze upon Christ. The figure of speech is that of the stadium and the foot race. All those worthies who triumphed "by faith," from the days of Abel and Enoch and Noah to those of the Maccabees, rise tier above tier as spectators, looking down upon us as we struggle along the course. However, the word "witnesses" means, not "those who see," but "those who testify." We hear their shouts. They are telling us of the power of faith.

Therefore we must "lay aside every weight," not merely things that are wrong, but anything which impedes our progress in the Chrisitian life. More obviously we must put aside every form of sin, which like a clinging garment "doth so easily beset us," encumbering us, preventing freedom of action, threatening to trip us and make us fall.

"Let us run with patience the race that is set before us" is the sum and substance of the appeal. To this all the other parts are subordinate. We are not to think of our fatigue, nor of the possibility of failure. We are not to envy those whose struggles seem less severe, whose victories are more easily won. We are not to seek for a smoother, shorter course to the crown. We are to endure, undaunted, undismayed, confident of success.

There is one absolute condition of victory: "Looking unto Jesus." He and not the heroes of old is our supreme Exemplar. "Looking away" from all others unto him seems to be the force of the words. He is the "author," not the Source, but the Leader, the Pioneer, and the "perfecter of our faith." In him faith found its perfect expression.

This supreme pattern of faith is seen in that he looked unto the unseen, he believed God's promises, he fixed his heart upon the unselfish "joy that was set before him"—

the joy of serving others, the joy of becoming the Redeemer of the world. Therefore he "endured the cross," not only its anguish and torture but its ignominy and digrace, "despising shame." Yet faith never loses its reward. He has been highly exalted, and now he is seated "at the right hand of the throne of God." Inspired by such an example, listening to the testimony of such a great "cloud of witnesses," we should be enabled to "lay aside every weight, and the sin which doth so easily beset us," and to "run with patience the race that is set before us."

D. THE TRIALS OF THE CHRISTIAN LIFE
Ch. 12:3-13

3 For consider him that hath endured such gainsaying of sinners against himself, that ye wax not weary, fainting in your souls. 4 Ye have not yet resisted unto blood, striving against sin: 5 and ye have forgotten the exhortation which reasoneth with you as with sons,

My son, regard not lightly the chastening of the Lord,
Nor faint when thou art reproved of him;
6 For whom the Lord loveth he chasteneth,
And scourgeth every son whom he receiveth.

7 It is for chastening that ye endure; God dealeth with you as with sons; for what son is there whom his father chasteneth not? 8 But if ye are without chastening, whereof all have been made partakers, then are ye bastards, and not sons. 9 Furthermore, we had the fathers of our flesh to chasten us, and we gave them reverence: shall we not much rather be in subjection unto the Father of spirits, and live? 10 For they indeed for a few days chastened us as seemed good to them; but he for our profit, that we may be partakers of his holiness. 11 All chastening seemeth for the present to be not joyous but grievous; yet afterward it yieldeth peaceable fruit unto them that have been exercised thereby, even the fruit of righteousness. 12 Wherefore lift up the hands that hang down, and the palsied knees; 13 and make straight paths for your feet, that that which is lame be not turned out of the way, but rather be healed.

Jesus has been pointed out as the great Exemplar of faith. His followers have been urged to fix their eyes upon him. They are now told to "consider" the opposition and "gainsaying" he endured for sinful men. They are to compare his experiences with their own. This will keep them from becoming weary and faint-hearted. It will inspire them to steadfastness and courage.

Such a comparison with the sufferings of Christ will have this result for two reasons: first, his followers will realize how much greater were his trials than theirs; second, they will be reminded that these very trials can be overruled for their eternal good.

In contrast with the cross and the death of Christ, the readers are told, "Ye have not yet resisted unto blood, striving against sin." The sin was that of unbelief and apostasy, to which they were being driven by the opposition and malice and scorn of their enemies. However much they had endured, not yet had they suffered martyrdom. Evidently, then, the readers were not in Jerusalem or in Rome, for in these cities Christians had already sealed with blood their witness to their Lord. These believers, then, should "wax not weary" nor be found "fainting" in their "souls."

In the second place, they should be encouraged by the fact that their persecution might be regarded as a fatherly discipline at the hands of God. This classic section must not be regarded as a complete solution of the problem of suffering. After all has been said, there is a mystery in pain. One is not to conclude that God is the author of evil, nor that pain is always punishment, nor that suffering is a proof of sin. It must be remembered that the "chastening" of these readers is being compared with the sufferings of Christ. He was sinless, and "though he was a Son, yet learned obedience by the things which he suffered; and having been made perfect, he became . . . the author of eternal salvation."

What the writer means to indicate is that opposition

and persecution and contempt, if endured with steadfast faith, may be overruled for the development of character and the perfecting of the soul. Indeed, all suffering can be so overruled, and in this sense can be regarded as an instrument used by a loving Father in the training and discipline of his child.

This fact the readers were tempted to disregard, and of it they were reminded by a quotation from The Proverbs: "Ye have forgotten the exhortation which reasoneth with you as with sons,

"My son, regard not lightly the chastening of the Lord,
Nor faint when thou art reproved of him;
For whom the Lord loveth he chasteneth,
And scourgeth every son whom he receiveth."

Nothing of harshness or cruelty or arbitrary infliction of pain is to be associated with this quotation, nor to be implied by the words of the writer. It is only the overruling love of God that he has in mind.

"It is for chastening," or with a view to moral development, "that ye endure; God dealeth with you as with sons." If God did not use our trials and sufferings for such high and holy purposes, he would be treating us with indifference, as though we were not his true children.

We have shown respect and honor to our earthly parents in their imperfect attempt to train us for life. "Shall we not much rather" accept humbly the providential discipline of our heavenly Father, who is using all these untoward and bitter experiences to secure our eternal good and to make us "partakers of his holiness"?

It is true that all discipline, "all chastening seemeth for the present to be not joyous but grievous." Christians are not asked to rejoice because of their sufferings, but in spite of them, and only in view of the blessings in which God can cause them to result. He can produce the fruit of peace and purity out of persecution and opposition and pain.

Such being the possible outcome of their sufferings, the

readers are urged to put aside all faintheartedness and fear, to "lift up the hands that hang down, and the palsied knees," and to keep unswervingly to the road that leads to the Promised Land. They are to encourage those of their number who are wavering and infirm, "that that which is lame be not turned out of the way, but rather be healed." Those who have found relief by submitting to the loving discipline of God are best able to soothe and strengthen others in weakness and distress.

E. THE NECESSITY OF PEACE AND PURITY
Ch. 12:14-17

14 Follow after peace with all men, and the sanctification without which no man shall see the Lord: 15 looking carefully lest there be any man that falleth short of the grace of God; lest any root of bitterness springing up trouble you, and thereby the many be defiled; 16 lest there be any fornicator, or profane person, as Esau, who for one mess of meat sold his own birthright. 17 For ye know that even when he afterward desired to inherit the blessing, he was rejected; for he found no place for a change of mind in his father, though he sought it diligently with tears.

In their conflict with the world, believers have been urged to be courageous and also to help their weaker brethren. Now they are urged to be not only helpful but harmonious: "Follow after peace with all men," with friend and foe alike, as far as in you lies. For peace almost anything may be sacrificed, but not purity. Christians must "follow after peace," but also must seek "the sanctification," the priestly consecration and growth in holiness, "without which no man shall see the Lord." This latter experience includes a present spiritual vision, but seems to point to the blessed beholding of Christ as he appears in glory, when "we shall be like him," when "we shall see him even as he is."

Likewise, Christians must watch over one another with

jealous care, "lest there be any man that falleth short of the grace of God," lest by apostasy there be any defection from their company and anyone fail to attain the blessedness which the grace of God offers.

One wicked man among many, like a poisonous "root," might spring up and spread his corrupt influence through the church, "and thereby the many be defiled."

They must not be led astray by any sensualist, or worldly-minded, unspiritual, "profane" man like Esau. For a mere mess of pottage he bartered away his birthright. He was a fit warning to these readers who were continually tempted to secure safety and relief from persecution by parting with their Christian faith. The warning is emphasized by pointing to the fate of Esau: "When he afterward desired to inherit the blessing, he was rejected; for he found no place for a change of mind in his father, though he sought it diligently with tears." His was the example of one who made an irrevocable and fatal choice. The deed could not be undone. The past was irreparable. So if one of these readers, under the allurements of the world or the pressure of temptation, should turn away from Christ the act could never be recalled. Such was the solemn warning against the forfeiting of heavenly prospects for worldly enjoyments.

F. A WARNING AGAINST REFUSING GOD'S VOICE   Ch. 12:18-29

18 For ye are not come unto a mount *that might be touched, and that burned with fire, and unto blackness, and darkness, and tempest, 19 and the sound of a trumpet, and the voice of words; which* voice *they that heard entreated that no word more should be spoken unto them;   20 for they could not endure that which was enjoined, If even a beast touch the mountain, it shall be stoned;   21 and so fearful was the appearance, that Moses said, I exceedingly fear and quake: 22 but ye are come unto mount Zion, and unto the city of the living God, the heavenly Jeru-*

salem, and to innumerable hosts of angels, 23 to the general assembly and church of the firstborn who are enrolled
in heaven, and to God the Judge of all, and to the spirits
of just men made perfect, 24 and to Jesus the mediator
of a new covenant, and to the blood of sprinkling that
speaketh better than that of Abel.   25 See that ye refuse
not him that speaketh.   For if they escaped not when they
refused him that warned them on earth, much more shall
not we escape who turn away from him that warneth from
heaven: 26 whose voice then shook the earth: but now
he hath promised, saying, Yet once more will I make to
tremble not the earth only, but also the heaven.   27 And
this word, Yet once more, signifieth the removing of those
things that are shaken, as of things that have been made,
that those things which are not shaken may remain.   28
Wherefore, receiving a kingdom that cannot be shaken,
let us have grace, whereby we may offer service well-pleasing to God with reverence and awe: 29 for our God is a
consuming fire.

The writer has just been speaking of the irrevocable
loss of a promised blessing.   It is a fit introduction to the
last great warning of the epistle, in which he contrasts the
old and the new covenants, and intimates the peril of bar-
tering the blessings of the new out of love for the old, the
danger of clinging to Moses while rejecting Christ, the
folly of lingering in the earthly Jerusalem and declining
citizenship in the heavenly Zion.

In this paragraph the argument of the epistle reaches
its climax.   The first parenthetic but essential warning was
against neglect.   (Ch. 2:1-4.)   The second was against
unbelief (chs. 3:7 to 4:13); the third against falling away
(chs. 5:11 to 6:20); the fourth against willful sin (ch.
10:26-31).   Here the warning is summarized in a single
sentence: "See that ye refuse not him that speaketh."   All
five are designed to carry out the supreme purpose of the
epistle, which is to secure loyalty to Christ and to prevent
the readers from turning away from him.

With this in view the writer gives this final comparison

of the two dispensations. As here presented, the old revealed the inaccessible nature of God and his unapproach-
able holiness; the new reveals his grace, which through
Christ provides access to God and fellowship and communion with him. To emphasize this contrast the writer
calls to mind the terrifying physical manifestations which
accompanied the revelation of God on Mt. Sinai, and the
spiritual and heavenly blessings now enjoyed by faith in
Christ. In memory he transports his readers to those
terrifying scenes which accompanied the giving of the Law.
They behold again the smoking, quaking mountain, the
"fire" and "blackness" and "darkness" and "tempest";
they hear the sounding "trumpet" and the unendurable
"voice." These, the writer implies, are the symbols of
that dispensation which is passing away.

Then the contrast is given: "Ye are come unto mount
Zion, and unto the city of the living God, the heavenly
Jerusalem." By fellowship with the King they already,
in effect, are in his eternal city. "Innumerable hosts of
angels" minister to them. They are in communion with
"the general assembly and church of the firstborn who
are enrolled in heaven"; they are in the immediate presence of God, the final "Judge of all"; they belong to the
blessed company of those who have been justified and
"made perfect" as worshipers by "Jesus the mediator of
a new covenant." His sprinkled blood speaks of cleansing and pardon, unlike the blood of Abel which cries from
the ground for vengeance.

Surely then, those who have already entered upon the
enjoyment of such blessings must not think of disregard-
ing this full and final revelation of God. They must "refuse not him that speaketh." For if they were severely
punished who disregarded the outward, visible, terrifying
manifestation of God, how "much more" severe must be
the penalty of those who disregard the heavenly message
sent through his Son.

That voice heard on Sinai was terrifying, causing the

earth to tremble; but Scripture predicts a more appalling shaking which will "make to tremble not the earth only, but also the heaven." This signifies a final, future testing, and the removal of all that is merely earthly and sensual and temporal, that the world of spiritual and heavenly realities "may remain."

Inasmuch, then, as we Christians belong to that heavenly and permanent order, since we are to inherit "a kingdom that cannot be shaken," let us seek to receive from God that grace which will enable us to render to him the humbler "service" of worshiping priests. Such service will be "well-pleasing to God." We should offer it in resignation to his will "with reverence and awe," as we regard his holiness. For, while he is full of mercy toward us, still "our God is a consuming fire."

G. DUTIES OF THE CHRISTIAN LIFE
Ch. 13:1-17

1. SOCIAL DUTIES   CH. 13:1-6

1 Let love of the brethren continue. 2 Forget not to show love unto strangers: for thereby some have entertained angels unawares. 3 Remember them that are in bonds, as bound with them; them that are ill-treated, as being yourselves also in the body. 4 Let marriage be had in honor among all, and let the bed be undefiled: for fornicators and adulterers God will judge. 5 Be ye free from the love of money; content with such things as ye have: for himself hath said, I will in no wise fail thee, neither will I in any wise forsake thee.
6 So that with good courage we say,
The Lord is my helper; I will not fear:
What shall man do unto me?

The last chapter is in substance a series of final exhortations to consistent Christian living. These exhortations are not all connected, yet they seem related to one temptation—the temptation to conceal one's Christian profession, to disregard fellow believers, to disown religious teachers, and to shun the hardship and the shame which might attend open allegiance to Christ.

The first group of these exhortations relates to the sphere of social life. Christians are to practice hospitality and charity, but to avoid impurity and greed. "Let love of the brethren continue," or, "Continue to cultivate brotherly love." Yet kindness is not to be limited to the circle of Christian friends; they must "forget not to show love unto strangers." Particularly in those early days of the church was hospitality a needful grace. Proper places of entertainment were difficult to secure, and Christians were continually journeying either as evangelists or to escape persecution or because of business pursuits. The exercise of this grace often brings unexpected blessings: "For thereby some have entertained angels unawares." This was literally true in the case of Abraham and Lot. Many of a later day have been surprised to find in humble guests veritable messengers of God.

"Remember," and so minister to your fellow believers who "are in bonds" as if you were in prison with them; and likewise be mindful of those who are "ill-treated" and persecuted, "as being yourselves also in the body" and therefore liable to similar treatment. "Let marriage be had in honor among all," and let its sanctity be kept inviolable, for those who desecrate the marriage bond will be overtaken, here and hereafter, by the judgments of God.

As frequently in Scripture, impurity and covetousness— impure love and a lust for gold—are here denounced at the same time: "Let marriage be had in honor" and "Be ye free from the love of money; content with such things as ye have." The basis of such contentment can be found in the promises of God, who has said, "I will in no wise fail thee, neither will I in any wise forsake thee." (See also Deut. 31:6, 8; Josh. 1:5.) In response to such an assurance of divine care, we Christians need not be anxious nor greedy of gain, but can express our confidence in God, using the joyful exclamation of the psalmist, quoted in the epistle,

> "The Lord is my helper; I will not fear:
> What shall man do unto me?"

2. RELIGIOUS DUTIES CH. 13:7-17

7 Remember them that had the rule over you, men that spake unto you the word of God; and considering the issue of their life, imitate their faith. 8 Jesus Christ is the same yesterday and to-day, yea and for ever. 9 Be not carried away by divers and strange teachings: for it is good that the heart be established by grace; not by meats, wherein they that occupied themselves were not profited. 10 We have an altar, whereof they have no right to eat that serve the tabernacle. 11 For the bodies of those beasts whose blood is brought into the holy place by the high priest as an offering for sin, are burned without the camp. 12 Wherefore Jesus also, that he might sanctify the people through his own blood, suffered without the gate. 13 Let us therefore go forth unto him without the camp, bearing his reproach. 14 For we have not here an abiding city, but we seek after the city which is to come. 15 Through him then let us offer up a sacrifice of praise to God continually, that is, the fruit of lips which make confession to his name. 16 But to do good and to communicate forget not: for with such sacrifices God is well pleased. 17 Obey them that have the rule over you, and submit to them: for they watch in behalf of your souls, as they that shall give account; that they may do this with joy, and not with grief: for this were unprofitable for you.

To the social duties before mentioned the writer now adds certain obligations as to personal religious life. His readers must remember the former teachers of the church, and imitate their faith in Christ and their willingness to suffer for his sake. They must be thankful to God, kind to their fellowmen, and loyal to their spiritual leaders.

Cherish an inspiring memory of "them that had the

rule over you," those noble teachers whose whole lives centered in their proclamation of the gospel, to whom you are indebted for your knowledge of "the word of God."

Bear in mind how they ended their lives, with what fortitude and courage they met persecution and death, and "imitate their faith." Their Savior is your Savior: "Jesus Christ is the same yesterday and to-day, yea and for ever." He who was worthy of their trust and sacrifice is worthy of yours. He who sustained and strengthened them will be your Support and Deliverer, now and evermore.

Be loyal to this changeless Christ. Do not be led away by false and novel teachings. Instead of being thus "carried away," "it is good that the heart be established" by the grace which God has bestowed in the gospel. We should place no dependence upon those sacrificial feasts from which those who scrupulously attend have derived no profit.

We Christians "have an altar"—the cross of Christ and the saving benefits of his death. From the benefits of this altar those are excluded who "serve the tabernacle," who still trust in rites and ceremonies, and who have rejected the Savior whom God has sent. This exclusion was pictured by the ancient ritual of the Jews. On the great Day of Atonement the bodies of those animals whose blood was carried by the high priest into the Holy Place were burned outside the camp. Neither the priests nor the worshipers could partake of their flesh. So the sacrifice of Christ was offered outside the gate of the Holy City. Indeed he was surrendered by his people into the hands of the Gentiles. This divine offering was thus not associated with the ritual of Moses and the Law. Those who adhere for salvation to the system of Judaism therefore do not share in the benefits of the cross and the death of Christ.

"Let us therefore go forth unto him without the camp, bearing his reproach." To be loyal to him usually means separation. It often involves the loss of friends and the acceptance of reproach and shame. It is like leaving the city of our birth, but it results in entering the city of God. The earthly Jerusalem is but a symbol of all the changing, temporary, imperfect religions of earth. "The Jerusalem that is above" is the embodiment of all that is spiritual, glorious, eternal. We can be patient in all the losses and separations of time, for we belong to eternity. "We have not here an abiding city, but we seek after the city which is to come."

We partake of the blessings of the perfect Sacrifice. For this very reason there are offerings which we must bring, the offerings of praise to God and of loving service to our fellowmen. If offered in the name of Christ, and with trust in him, these offerings are pleasing to God. "Through him then," says the writer, "let us offer up a sacrifice of praise to God continually"; and, "To do good and to communicate forget not: for with such sacrifices God is well pleased."

Not only are Christians to hold in loving remembrance Christian leaders of the past, but they are to be obedient to those of the present: "Obey them that have the rule over you, and submit to them." The reasons for such an exhortation are then mentioned. The first is the serious responsibility of these leaders. They are like wakeful shepherds who some day will render to the Chief Shepherd an account of their service. They are to be so obeyed that they may discharge their task "with joy, and not with grief," or with the groanings of one who is burdened with thankless and distressing duties. The second reason for obedience to Christian leaders is that a contrary course only results in personal loss: "For this were unprofitable for you."

III
CONCLUSION
Ch. 13:18-25

A. A REQUEST FOR PRAYER   Ch. 13:18-19

18 Pray for us: for we are persuaded that we have a good conscience, desiring to live honorably in all things. 19 And I exhort you the more exceedingly to do this, that I may be restored to you the sooner.

As is not unusual in the New Testament letters, the closing section of the epistle contains a request for prayer: "Pray for us," or, "Continue to remember me in your prayers." Two reasons for perseverance in prayer are given. The first is the assurance of the conscious integrity of the writer. It is difficult to pray for one whose motives are insincere or whose conduct is in question. The writer, however, can say of himself, "We are persuaded that we have a good conscience, desiring to live honorably in all things."

Another encouragement is given in the form of the specific and personal character of the request which the writer makes. It is well to say, "Pray for us"; but how much easier it is to grant that petition when some definite desire or need is mentioned. "That I may be restored to you the sooner" is the longing of his heart, which he hopes may be realized in answer to the supplication of his friends. The very words imply that there is true affection uniting his heart with theirs and that he is certain of their earnest intercession and confident of their love.

B. THE BENEDICTION   Ch. 13:20-21

20 Now the God of peace, who brought again from the dead the great shepherd of the sheep with the blood of an eternal covenant, even our Lord Jesus, 21 make you perfect in every good thing to do his will, working in us that which is well-pleasing in his sight, through Jesus Christ; to whom be the glory for ever and ever.   Amen.

The writer has asked for the prayers of his friends.   He now prays for them, and his prayer is in the form of one of the most beautiful and inclusive benedictions that the Scriptures contain.   The prayer is addressed to "the God of peace," and while peace is an attribute of God the phrase is here intended to remind us that God is the Source of peace, and that he has secured perfect peace with himself and for his people.   This he has done by the mission and work of Christ, who is here called "the great shepherd of the sheep," and is thus designated as the one who fulfills all that is set forth by "the sweet psalmist of Israel" in his matchless Shepherd Psalm.   He has been "brought again from the dead" and has entered the Holy Place on high in virtue of his atoning death, by which he sealed "an eternal covenant" between God and his people.   Their salvation is absolutely assured.   There is need of no other sacrifice, no other offering, no other priest, no other intercession.   The prayer of the writer is that God will perfectly equip the readers to serve him, granting them every grace that they may need for the doing of his will, and producing in them "that which is well-pleasing in his sight."   This is to be done, this can be done, only "through Jesus Christ," to whom is ascribed everlasting glory and praise.

C. PERSONAL MESSAGES   Ch. 13:22-25

22 But I exhort you, brethren, bear with the word of exhortation: for I have written unto you in few words.   23 Know ye that our brother Timothy hath been set at liberty; with whom, if he come shortly, I will see you.

24 Salute all them that have the rule over you, and all the saints. They of Italy salute you.
25 Grace be with you all. Amen.

In a personal postscript the writer appeals to his readers to give serious heed to his exhortation, which he declares he has conveyed "in few words." To some modern readers this "exhortation," which means this epistle, must appear rather lengthy. Length, however, is relative. It depends largely upon the importance of the matter in hand. If Christ is the only Savior, if he is the complete and final Revelation of God to man, if through him real and immediate access to God is possible, then an exhortation to those in peril of turning away from Christ might seem to the writer all too brief, however extended such a warning might be.

The welcome news is added that Timothy, best known to the church as the close and beloved friend of the apostle Paul, has been set free from imprisonment. Surely he was in no danger of apostasy. He had learned what it was to "suffer hardship . . . as a good soldier of Christ Jesus." If he reaches the writer of the letter in a short time, they will together visit the friends to whom the letter is addressed.

Greetings are sent to the church officers and to all their fellow Christians. Nor were these greetings only on the part of the writer. "They of Italy" unite in sending these messages of affection and esteem. Who were these Italian friends? They were either Christians residing in Italy, or, more probably, Italians absent from their native land who were sending salutations to their brethren at home. However, the phrase gives no certain indication as to the place of writing or as to the destination of the letter.

The final benediction, in its liturgical form, indicates that the letter was intended to be read aloud at public worship. It is in essence a prayer that God's blessing may rest upon those who are addressed: "Grace be with you all. Amen."